Mountain Biking
Washington

Mountain Biking
Washington

Gordon Black

FALCON®

HELENA, MONTANA

A **FALCON** GUIDE ®

Falcon® Publishing is continually expanding its list of recreation guidebooks. All books include detailed descriptions, accurate maps, and all the information necessary for enjoyable trips. You can order extra copies of this book and get information and prices for other Falcon® guidebooks by writing Falcon, P.O. Box 1718, Helena, MT 59624 or calling toll free 1-800-582-2665. Also, please ask for a free copy of our current catalog. Visit our website at www.Falcon.com or contact us by e-mail at falcon@falcon.com.

© 1999 by Falcon® Publishing, Inc., Helena, Montana
Printed in the United States of America.

1 2 3 4 5 6 7 8 9 0 MG 04 03 02 01 00 99

Falcon and FalconGuide are registered trademarks of Falcon® Publishing, Inc.

All photos by author unless otherwise noted.

Library of Congress Cataloging-in-Publication Data

Black, Gordon, 1957-
   Mountain biking Washington / by Gordon Black.
        p.   cm.— (A FalconGuide)
   Includes index.
   ISBN 1-56044-806-7 (pbk.)
   1. All terrain cycling—Washington (State) Guidebooks. 2. Bicycle trails—Washington (State) Guidebooks. 3. Washington (State) Guidebooks. I. Title
II. Series: Falcon guide.
GV1045.5.W2B53   1999
917.9704'43—dc21   99-25894
                                                                                      CIP

CAUTION

Outdoor recreational activities are by their very nature potentially hazardous. All participants in such activities must assume the responsibility for their own actions and safety. The information contained in this guidebook cannot replace sound judgment and good decision-making skills, which help reduce risk exposure, nor does the scope of this book allow for disclosure of all the potential hazards and risks involved in such activities.

Learn as much as possible about the outdoor recreational activities in which you participate, prepare for the unexpected, and be cautious. The reward will be a safer and more enjoyable experience.

♻ Text pages printed on recycled paper.

To Francie, whose enthusiasm for all things wild, peaceful, and beautiful is matched only by her skills as an editor, coach, and all around swell gal.

Acknowledgments

Any book is a collaborative effort, even if it's only the author's name that goes on the front. Putting together close to sixty rides in a year required the cooperation of many individuals who provided tips on places to ride, fact-checked my write-ups, and generally helped ensure that my time spent researching rides was productive. I am especially grateful to the recreation specialists who work for the US Forest Service, especially those at the following ranger districts: Republic and Sullivan Lake, Colville National Forest; Cle Elum and Leavenworth, Wenatchee National Forest; Cowlitz Valley and Mt. Adams, Gifford Pinchot National Forest; Hood Canal, Quilcene, Quinault, and Soleduck, Olympic National Forest; Twisp, Okanogan National Forest; North Bend and White River, Mt. Baker-Snoqualmie National Forest.

Their local knowledge and willingness to check over write-ups was a great assistance to me. To all the rangers around the state who work on helping the public enjoy our wonderful forests, I doff my helmet. And an equal thanks goes to the folks at the Department of Natural Resources, who work diligently to provide public access while fulfilling the agency's primary mission of sustaining the trust accounts held for schools, colleges, and universities.

I'll count myself among the ranks of mountain bikers who owe a special thanks to the unpaid advocates who turn up at public meetings and work behind the scenes to ensure continued access on the state's trails. Foremost among them are the members of the Backcountry Bicycle Trails Club and founding president Walt Shostak. Ditto those willing to put their labor into maintaining or creating trails. Keep up the good work.

Mountain biking is a social activity and I'd like to acknowledge the companions who have accompanied me on outings, and tolerated with good humor the frequent stops necessary in collecting data on a trail. They include Walt Cannon, Jay Robertson, Suzanne Schleder, and Ken Gillis.

Lastly, a special thank you to my partner Francie Petracca whose numerous talents extend to map-making, proof-reading, and providing moral support for this project—even as we built a house the same summer.

Great care has been taken to ensure that the rides in this book are as they are described, but trail conditions and access roads can be affected by a number of factors, especially the weather. Before you embark on a long drive to one of the rides included here, please take the wise precaution of calling ahead to a ranger station or other appropriate land manager. Checking in advance is the first step to having a good time.

Happy trails to you.

Contents

Map Legend

Interstate		Campground	
U.S. Highway		Picnic Area	
State or Other Principal Road		Buildings	
Forest Road		Peak/Elevation	4,507 ft.
Interstate Highway		Bridge/Pass	
Paved Road		Gate	
Gravel Road		Parking Area	
Unimproved Road		Boardwalk/Pier	
Trail (singletrack)		Railroad Track	
Trailhead		Cliffs/Bluff	
Trail Marker		Power Line	
Waterway		Forest Boundary	
Intermittent Waterway		Map Orientation	
Lake/Reservoir		Scale	0 0.5 1 MILES
Meadow/Swamp			

Statewide Locator Map

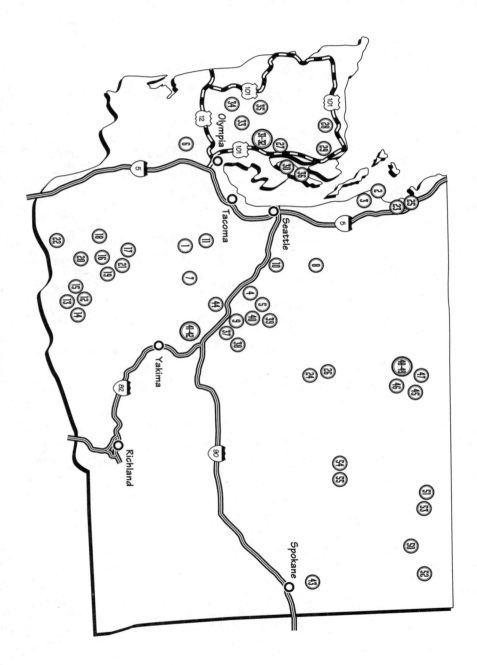

Introduction

The raw forces of nature conspired to create a little bit of mountain bike nirvana in the upper left corner of the United States. The giant plates in the earth's crust that thrust upwards started shaping things nicely, as if anticipating mountain bikes. That was about 50 million years ago in the Olympic Mountains and 5 to 6 million years ago in the Cascade Mountains. Of course, all this movement that geologists call plate subduction has a habit of creating ragged and beautiful peaks that you can barely climb with ropes, far less ride up. That's why bikers owe gratitude to the glaciers that slip-slid their way through much later. They helped smooth out the valleys to lessen some of the steep slopes and create ridable uphills and wonderful freewheeling opportunities. The actual invention of the freewheel came about 21,000 years after the glaciers began their work, but who's counting?

The sum of this raw beauty of rock and ice activity, not to mention volcanoes, is that Washington state is well endowed with the type of terrain that makes for blissful mountain biking. The Cascade Mountains that run like a spine from British Columbia to Oregon give the state a dual personality— cooler, wet, and spongy on the west; hotter, dry, and chaparral-like on the east. Washington offers the gamut of riding experiences from sparse high desert to intensely green rain forest. Year-round riding is possible here when trail conditions permit. Let's emphasize that word permit. It's so easy to get carried away in the exhilaration of a singletrack trail or a downhill fire road that you can quickly forget that we often ride in fragile environments that deserve to be treated with respect. The vast majority of riding areas are on public lands; the vast majority of trails are shared with other users.

As an activity, mountain biking is still in its puberty. Compared to equestrian riding, hiking, or even offroad motorcycling, mountain biking and its practitioners are newcomers. As such, we may naturally display some adolescent impatience about trail use. After all, this fat-tire stuff is fun and we can't wait to whoop it up wherever the pavement ends. Collectively, we've all learned that such antics don't win us friends among the bridle or walking set. Public bodies, be they city, county, state, tribal, or federal, have no incentive to accommodate those whom they perceive as rowdies, and they have every incentive to retain the status quo. That's a long-winded way of saying: Please practice militant politeness and courtesy on the trails. The route you keep open might just be your favorite. Or it might be mine.

Thirteen years ago mountain bikers in Southern California faced a series of closures of their favorite riding areas. Officialdom, responding to complaints by hikers and equestrians of dangerous and inconsiderate behavior by mountain bikers, wanted to close a number of trails to bikes. Seeing this threat, a group of riders began to organize and talk to park rangers about the problems mountain bikes were allegedly (and actually) causing. There were stories of spooked horses, gates left open, trail erosion, collisions, near-misses, rudeness, and excessive speed. Through dialog, opponents and officials began to look at possible solutions. Hiker, equestrian, and mountain bike groups worked together so that all could enjoy the trails. Those discussions resulted in some trail closures to mountain bikes, especially where trails were very narrow and had many blind corners, but fewer outright bans. Mountain bikers accepted those as a reasonable compromise.

By now, you've probably heard of the International Mountain Biking Association (IMBA) code of conduct. Read it (its on page 9), know it, and follow it. Responsible mountain bikers, worried about the renegade image of the sport, developed the code. In Washington, the Backcountry Bicycle Trails Club (BBTC) and others have done a great job of promoting responsible trail use and representing the interests of mountain bikers before public bodies. Despite the best efforts of BBTC, King County Parks still banned mountain bikes from the old truck roads inside Cougar Regional Park. The club didn't even argue to keep open the trails to mountain bikes, yet it still lost. This may be a timely reminder about making assumptions. Don't assume a trail you ride tomorrow will necessarily remain open to mountain bikers next year. Likewise, while every ride listed in this guide was legally open at the time of publication of this guidebook, conditions may have changed.

One of the most exciting trails in the North Cascades, Devil's Gulch near Wenatchee, is not included in this guidebook because at the time of researching that area the trail was under threat of closure because of logging. Only significant opposition from mountain bikers resulted in the Wenatchee National Forest officials relenting and promising to retain the trail. (If you plan to ride the trail, contact the Leavenworth Ranger Station for details, or visit a bike store in Wenatchee. The trail is hardly a secret.)

Trails close for other reasons, too. Housing or road development, floods, loss of bridges, lack of maintenance, and public opposition. We can't control the weather; we don't write the budgets; and it seems unlikely that we can prevent timber contracts or development. But we do have power over public perception. Be good and you'll be treated nicely. Most of the time.

One of the great attractions of public lands in the United States is the virtually unrestricted access to them. Approximately 45 percent of Washington is in public ownership—lands administered by federal agencies, the state's Department of Natural Resources (DNR), and municipal authorities. National forests, which comprise more than 8 million acres, are the main source of rides in this guide, but the DNR, which holds about 3 million acres in trust, also offers great places to spin your wheels. While budgets for recreational trails are under pressure or diminishing, that doesn't mean trails have to be closed. Both the USDA Forest Service and the DNR work with volunteer groups willing to build or maintain trails. Such groups, as well as other important numbers, are listed in the Appendix at the back of this guide. If you can give up a day of riding to wield a shovel, you'll be making a worthy contribution to your own future riding pleasure.

Mountain biking is here to stay. In bike stores, mountain bikes substantially outsell traditional road bikes. Few other sports have become so hugely popular as quickly as mountain biking. It's already gained the accolade of the Olympic Games. But to truly enjoy this activity, it has to be experienced in the great outdoors. We hope this guide provides you with useful information about some of the areas in this state to explore and enjoy. Before you reach for your maps, get familiar with the following preparations.

TWO'S COMPANY, THREE IS BETTER

Many rides in this guide are in remote forested areas with difficult or very limited road access. Good preparation of your mind, body, and bike are essential so that you never have to test the abilities of the local rescue team. Professional and volunteer rescue crews quite naturally get testy when they end up rescuing someone ill-prepared for the great outdoors. If your ride is in a mountainous area—and many are—prepare for mountain weather. Don't assume that because it's sunny and warm at the parking lot that it won't be hailing, snowing, or raining at the pass. Carry enough gear to keep you warm, especially in the spring or fall when weather can change rapidly. Always ride with a buddy or two. Even experienced riders can take a spill and medical help may be needed—a riding partner can raise the alarm. Try to let someone else know where you are going and what time you plan on returning.

DRESS FOR COMFORT

Riding shorts with a padded crotch area are a must for a long day in the saddle. Ditto, padded gloves will help prevent your meridian nerve from causing numbness in your hands. Close-fitting tights are good for cool days or long descents. A riding jersey is cut long in the back for a reason—to keep your kidneys and lower back protected from cold. A long T-shirt may also do the job but may become damp and unpleasant when saturated with sweat. Shoes must have stiff soles to prevent foot fatigue. Eyewear keeps objects such as tree branches or insects out of your orbs.

IT'S ALL IN YOUR HEAD

Hairpin bends. Rocks. Roots. Steep inclines. Low branches. Slippery leaves. Holes. Ruts. Falls. Slips. Spills. Head-over-handlebars. Face plants. Spin-outs. Cranial nerves. Forebrain. Cerebellum. Hemorrhage. Permanent injury. Helmet. 'Nuff said?

TRAIL MEDICINE

It is surprisingly easy to scrape an elbow or a knee, get stung by a wasp or have dust blow into your eyes while out riding. Those are normal hazards. Preparing for them by carrying a basic first-aid kit will ensure that these minor annoyances remain just that. Make up a kit with such items as scissors, bandages, headache pills, eye wash, surgical tape, cortisone, rubber gloves, and sunscreen, or purchase one of the excellent field first-aid kits available from outdoor equipment retailers.

THE ROAD TO NOWHERE

As accurate as our guide maps try to be they are no substitute for topographic maps. However, trails can change so quickly that maps are often out of date by the time they are issued. Indeed, you'll find most maps published by the United States Geological Survey (USGS) to be of limited value for trail location because they are updated so infrequently. However, they are indispensable for basic navigation and for showing topographic detail, such as elevations, rivers, and mountains. Publishing outfits such as Green Trails, Custom Correct, and others use the USGS data and then produce current maps that show trails. Green Trails maps are based on 15-minute intervals derived from the USGS, the Forest Service, and other sources. These also show contours and, since they are designed primarily for recreational use, clearly indicate trails and all kinds of roads. Trail distances are marked. Unfortunately, Green Trails maps do not show active or abandoned railways, the latter a major omission for mountain bikers. This does mean that the hundreds of miles of logging railroads that formerly laced through the woods are unrepresented on these maps. Green Trails' coverage is limited to the most popular hiking areas in the Cascades and Olympics. Some forests produce and sell (typically for $3 to $4) excellent ranger district maps that contain contour shading, and all have complete forest maps.

Remember, though, that just because a trail is printed on a map doesn't necessarily mean it is still open. Landslides, floods, and logging may have altered the landscape the trail traverses. While maps may not be able to document recent events, they remain an essential part of your mountain biking equipment.

Of course, any map is only as useful as the person using it. If you're unsure about map-reading, consider taking a basic class in navigation. It will go a long way toward ensuring safe and rewarding backcountry travel by mountain bike. I know riders who also take along a compass. While it is not essential for following the trails laid out in this book, it sure doesn't hurt to carry one with you. Likewise, there may be a time in the near future when handlebar-mounted GPS (global position satellites) units are as common as computers are now.

The Forest Service also produces travel maps, normally issued free. These show restrictions due to logging or weather closures. They also list hunting seasons, which may influence your decision to ride in a certain area at a particular time of year. The Forest Service also produces folding maps (typically costing around $4) that show all Forest Service roads but do not have the current information contained in travel maps. It's worth noting that the Forest Service has now renumbered all its roads in Washington forests. This makes life considerably easier. For example, FR 25 in the Gifford Pinchot National Forest is a main travel road with side roads which are then numbered as a suffix of 25, such as FR 2504.

A number of counties are covered in maps produced by Metsker. Again, these can be useful but are frequently out of date. Custom Correct Maps, a small company in Port Angeles, makes maps that show good detail of popular areas in and around Olympic National Park.

Map sources are listed with each ride, plus there are main Forest Service offices listed in the Appendix. Remember too, that nature can quickly make maps obsolete by changing river routes, causing landslides, and other events that will render the information out of date.

BEWARE THE BONK

The bonk occurs when the sugar levels in your blood drop to such a degree during exercise that you stop thinking straight, feel tired, but still keep going. A rider experiencing the bonk will often be unable to make good decisions on technically challenging trails. If you're planning a ride estimated to take 3 to 5 hours, bring along enough food to replenish spent calories. Snacks packed with concentrated energy-giving foods are compact, easy to carry, and will quickly restore a sagging rider. Popular brands include PowerBar and ClifBar but there are many others that may better meet your taste requirements.

Don't wait too long before eating. Good preparation includes having eaten an appropriately generous amount before you embark.

COOL, CLEAR WATER

A pint bottle of water weighs just over a pound. During strenuous exercise, like riding up a steep hill on a hot day, you should drink at least a pint per hour. All good-quality mountain bikes come with places to carry at least two 26-ounce bottles. A clutch of ingenious manufacturers now also offers 60- and 90-ounce bladders held in backpack-like devices. These are great because you drink from a tube without removing your hands from the bars. Unless you carry a water filter, don't even consider using streams as a source of rehydration. Our little parasitic friends can inhabit apparently clear mountain water. The best policy is to carry the water you'll need with you. As a careful rider, you will want to fill your bottles from the kitchen tap, rather than trust that trailheads will have potable water.

TRAILSIDE MECHANICS

The side of the trail is no place to undertake what should be scheduled maintenance of your mount. If you're heading out for the day, make sure your bike is ready for it. Tighten nuts, lube the chain, inflate tires, that sort of thing. A well-prepared bike is less likely to give you trouble. That said, mechanical problems can arise. On one ride my rear derailleur folded around my freewheel, breaking the chain. I had climbed six miles uphill and didn't relish the idea of ending my outing prematurely. Luckily, I was carrying all the essential tools to make good the repair and spent the next three hours enjoying marvelous scenery with my riding companion.

Small, folding, lightweight toolkits that stash easily in a bag or a pocket will readily help you repair the most common mechanical problems. At a minimum you and your riding companion should have between you the following: pump; spare inner tube; glueless patches or patch kit; chain-link tool; spare chain link; range of Allen wrenches; flat blade and Phillips screwdrivers; spoke wrench; adjustable wrench; 8-10mm open wrenches. Slip a pair of latex gloves and a tiny tube of liquid soap (available from bike stores) into the kit to clean up your hands after repairs. These should help you correct 90 percent of mechanical glitches, but there are numerous other tools that it might be wise to carry. Obviously, any tool is only as good as the person who knows how to use it. If you don't know, take a class or pick up a book on bike maintenance and repair.

TRAILHEAD PARKING

Few things in life are free but tooling around in the mountains on your bike (or on foot) used to be one of them. Not anymore. Many national forests have adopted a policy of charging fees for trailhead parking. This typically costs $3 per day or $25 for an annual parking pass. These fees were introduced as an experiment in 1997. Judging from the volume of signs now erected at many forest-owned trailheads, this experiment seems certain to become a permanent feature of outdoor recreation. Funds raised from the parking fees are retained by the forest administrators for trail improvements. The issue is controversial in part because opponents believe that the trails should be maintained by the taxpayer dollars that are awarded to the Forest Service by Congress, without resorting to extra "user fees." If you're unhappy about the fees, write to your member of Congress and complain. You may also want to get in contact with any of several groups that have organized against the parking fees.

KNOW THYSELF

Don't push yourself beyond your own limits of endurance or strength. Recognize when the light is failing and you won't make your day's target destination. It's okay. Come back another day, rather than push yourself into exhaustion. Likewise, if a riding companion is not up to the same level of stamina, recognize his limits and turn around. Read the weather as well. Are black clouds gathering near the mountaintop you're heading to? The wise rider will head home.

LOVE MOTHER EARTH, AND HIKERS

There is a reason why we choose to seek out quiet trails with mountain views and actual wildlife. Mountain biking is not a video game, it's the real thing. That means you have to do your bit to take care of things. Like respecting the trail by not skidding downhill, creating shortcuts, cutting corners, and otherwise damaging the unpaved byways. Tread lightly, if at all. Sometimes a trail is too wet to ride without damaging it, especially in western Washington. Find out in advance by calling the land manager. When trails are ridable, other people may be using them. A smile and a hello are always welcome gestures to any trail user. Slow down to walking pace when encountering hikers; stop entirely for horses. Equines are noble beasts, very large and prone to skittish behavior. Veteran equestrians may have trouble controlling a horse scared by your Lycra-clad presence, and inexperienced riders certainly will. Make eye contact—with the rider, not the horse—and await his or her instructions to pass. Equestrians are becoming accustomed to meeting bikers on the trails, but treat each encounter as if it were your first. Each horse and rider is different. Hikers and horse riders will appreciate your consideration on the trail. Besides, those folks are enjoying the outdoors and you shouldn't spoil their favorite activity. Embrace these limitations as the price of sustained access to riding places and the continued pursuit of your personal pleasure.

Happy trails to you.

Remember, there are riders of all abilities out there. They have the same right to fun as you do.

IMBA Rules of the Trail

The International Mountain Bicycling Association (IMBA) is a non-profit advocacy organization dedicated to promoting mountain biking that's environmentally sound and socially responsible. IMBA's work keeps trails open and in good condition for everyone.

These rule of the trail are reprinted with permission from IMBA.

1. Ride on open trails only. Respect trail and road closures (ask if not sure), avoid possible trespass on land, obtain permits and authorization as may be required. Federal and state wilderness areas are closed to cycling. The way you ride will influence trail management decisions and policies.

2. Leave no trace. Be sensitive to the dirt beneath you. Even on open (legal) trails avoid riding immediately after heavy rains or when the trail surface is soft and muddy. In some locations, muddy trails are unavoidable. Recognize different types of soils and trail construction. Practice low impact cycling. This also means staying on existing trails and not creating new ones. Be sure to pack out at least as much as you pack in.

3. Control your bicycle. Inattention for even a second can cause problems. Obey all bicycle speed regulations and recommendations.

4. Always yield trail. Give your fellow trail users plenty of advance notice when you're approaching. A friendly greeting (or bell) is considerate and works well; don't startle others. Show your respect when passing by, slowing to a walking pace or even stopping, particularly when you meet horses. Anticipate other trail users around corners or in blind spots.

5. Don't scare animals. All animals are startled by an unannounced approach, a sudden movement, or a loud noise. This can be dangerous for you, others, and the animals. Give animals extra room and time to adjust to you. When passing horses use special care and follow the directions from the horseback riders (ask if uncertain). Running cattle and disturbing wildlife is a serious offense. Leave gates as you found them, or as marked.

6. Plan ahead. Know your equipment, your ability, and the area in which you are riding—and prepare accordingly. Be self-sufficient at all times, keep your equipment in good repair, and carry all necessary supplies for changes in weather or other conditions. A well-executed trip is a satisfaction to you and not a burden or offense to others. Always wear a helmet and appropriate safety gear.

Keep trails open by setting a good example of environmentally sound and socially responsible off-road cycling.

If you have any questions or comments, you can contact IMBA at:
IMBA
P.O. Box 7578
Boulder, CO 80306-7578
Tel: (303) 545-9011
Fax: (303) 545-9026
http://www.imba.com/

About this Book

The rides included in this guidebook are a representation of the type of trails available for mountain biking in Washington state. This is not the definitive selection of rides in the state. That would take several volumes and several years of research. And besides, by the time the last ride was completed who knows what condition the trails ridden earlier would be in. In selecting rides for inclusion I have attempted to provide a good mix of easy, moderate, and more challenging routes, as well as to give a good geographic spread.

A significant majority of the rides are on public lands—mainly in national forest, but also on lands owned by the state of Washington. While there are hundreds of thousands of acres owned by forest companies such as Weyerhaeuser, Simpson, Plum Creek, and Pope & Talbot, where public access is permitted, it is usually on a much more restricted basis than on public land. For instance, Weyerhaeuser often limits public access to weekends and major holidays when their workers are not present. Obtaining reliable maps of these private lands is also often difficult. A case in point is the hour or more I spent in Aberdeen trying to locate a map of local Weyerhaeuser lands, finally tracking one down in a gun shop. For these reasons, I chose to leave out many rides on private lands.

After visiting several off-road vehicle recreation areas I've concluded that, for the most part, they don't make for great bicycling experiences. Ruts created by motorcycles tend to make for unpleasant cycling. Hence, there are but a couple of rides in this book that are in ORV areas. If you feel differently, I encourage you to visit ORV areas and enjoy the extensive trail networks that exist there.

I have bowed to the power of numbers: Most riders live around Puget Sound and can't always manage to drive three or more hours to enjoy a day's ride. You'll notice that a sizeable number of the rides are within two hours of the Seattle area. If I could have, I would have included the very best rides that you can get to without driving very far. Alas, the raw forces that conspired to create mountains and valleys also created Puget Sound and the surrounding topography. As population growth fills the gap between sound and mountains, the places we'd like to ride in (and used to ride in) are forever lost to tract housing, shopping malls, and suburban sprawl.

Shaping growth is a political issue beyond the scope of mountain-bike advocacy. But you can still do your part by supporting the tireless volunteers of local bike groups as they work to halt trail closures and encourage land managers to develop nearby places to ride. If you can't donate time to maintain trails or build new ones, at least dip into your wallet to help with these groups' expenses.

Lastly, don't be afraid of the dirt. Get out and explore new routes. Create a loop. This guidebook—and the other excellent volumes out there—should be your starting point for further mountain bike adventures.

Using this Guide

Each ride description in this book follows the same format, beginning with the number and name of the ride, followed by the "at-a-glance" information. This information is divided among the following headings:

Location: The general location of the ride, with distance and direction from the nearest town.

Distance: The length of the ride in miles, plus its configuration: loop, one-way, or out-and-back. Super-cyclists will ride the trails faster than mere mountain bikers (this author included).

Tread: Tread describes the trail surface, such as gravel, dirt, jeep road.

Time: An estimate of the time it takes to complete the ride. *The time listed is the actual riding time and does not include rest stops.* Strong, skilled riders may be able to complete the ride more quickly than the time listed. Less experienced riders may take considerably longer. Severe weather, trail conditions, or mechanical problems may prolong a ride. The estimated riding times are what I anticipate an average rider, tackling a trail within her ability, will take. Time has a habit of slipping by faster than a great downhill singletrack, so learn to trust the expected times. Give yourself kudos if you complete a trail faster than the estimate but always allow at least the amount of time stated.

Aerobic level: The level of physical fitness effort required to complete the ride. This is rated as easy, moderate, or strenuous. (See page 13 for an explanation of the rating system.)

Technical difficulty: The level of bike-handling skills required to complete the ride. Technical difficulty is rated on a scale of 1 to 5, with 1 being the easiest. (See page 13 for an explanation of the rating system.)

Best time to ride: The best time of the year to ride a particular trail. This takes into consideration such factors as weather and hunting seasons.

Facilities: Lists the availability of water and toilets.

Land status: List the land managing agency or the landowner.

Maps: A list of available maps. Most, but not all, areas are shown on official maps, including USGS maps.

Access: Detailed directions to the start of the ride.

Notes on the trail: A detailed description of the highlights (and low points) of a ride.

Who doesn't love a loop? Where possible, this guide includes loop routes but some simple out-and-backs are represented when a loop was not available or could not be devised. In a number of instances, loops have been developed specifically for inclusion in this guide. In other cases, included loops are established rides.

Trail names used in this guidebook are taken from USDA Forest Service and other maps or from their vernacular use. Where no previous name exists, I have devised one based on a major topographic feature of the ride, or mere whim. (Isn't that why there are "Soda Streams" and "Candy Mountains" all over the West?)

Rides that take place on Forest Service land—and that's the vast majority of them—include road numbers used on Forest Service maps. A quick primer on how the numbering system works: Each forest has a selection of mainline roads (the widest and most maintained) that are easily identifiable by their two digit numbers—for example, FR 22 in Colville National Forest. Secondary roads that branch off FR 22 incorporate the number of the mainline, such as FR 2220, FR 2212, etc. Other roads, known as spurs, have three digit numbers. Thus road 500 is a spur off FR 22, and so on. Roads with three digits can vary in quality considerably, from barely maintained to good condition.

The Ride: A mile-by-mile description of the ride to help you keep your bearings.

TRAIL RATING SYSTEM

Rating a trail is highly subjective. One hill-climb may prove easy to a veteran rider but very strenuous to a beginner. Likewise, obstacles that experienced mountain bikers roll over without a thought may be a ride-stopping blockage for someone else. Feedback from other riders tells me that it is better to have a trail rated more difficult than it proves to be, rather than the other way around. Nobody likes surprises of the energy-sapping kind. Accordingly, the trails in this book are rated by a combination of the IMBA system and the FalconGuide system.

AEROBIC RATING

It falls into three categories—easy, moderate, and strenuous.

Easy—Almost flat terrain or small hills not requiring sustained effort. These may be steep in places but will typically be no more than a half-mile long. Some people may choose to walk the short, steep sections. A trail rated easy is suitable for beginners and, in most cases, inexperienced riders and children.

Moderate—This is a wide category. Moderate aerobic ability translates into trails with hills that may be several miles long. Such trails will gain elevation at 50 to 200 feet per mile. Moderate also encompasses trails that have frequent short but steep hills.

Strenuous—The hardest category of ride. Strenuous rides require sustained aerobic activity on uphill sections. Rides rated this way include trails that gain more than 200 feet of elevation per mile for more than three miles. Some trails may have sections where the elevation gain is greater than 500 feet per mile. As a rule, most people cannot ride on slopes that rise more than 600 feet per mile, and cannot sustain such climbing for very far.

TECHNICAL RATING

The IMBA numeric system (1–5) has been adapted to rate the technical difficulty of rides in this guidebook.

1. Easiest trail with a largely smooth, rolling surface and few or no obstacles. Includes trails that may contain sections of gravel and the occasional twig or stick on the trail. Trail is predictable.

2. Largely obstacle-free trail that may have more sections of uneven surface, such as loose gravel, large rocks, or slippery surfaces. Trail route is mostly predictable.

3. Trail where rocks, roots, obstacles, and uneven surfaces are frequently interspersed with smoother, easier terrain. Trail likely twists and turns unexpectedly. Water is often an additional hazard on such trails.

4. Roots, logs, rocks, uneven surfaces, water, deep mud, and ruts abound. Such trails are technically challenging, requiring sustained concentration and quick responses to handle unexpected conditions. Trails receiving this rating are often on steep terrain involving tight switchbacks, dangerous drop-offs, and other high-risk hazards.

5. Every known hazard, including those extremely difficult to negotiate. Lots of trail obstacles that appear without warning, and constantly changing trail conditions. Trails include sections with a high level of risk of injury. Only the most skilled and adept riders should tackle trails with this rating.

For example a trail rated Moderate 4 may include a ride that does not require sustained hill-climbing but may have frequent short hills mixed with

A visitation by a butterfly is a sure sign of a great ride to come.

technically challenging terrain. Where a trail is rated with two numbers, such as 2–3 it means that it is largely a category 2 ride but also contains some technical sections that receive the higher (category 3) rating. If such technical areas constituted more than 20-percent of the ride, it would be rated a straight category 3.

ELEVATIONS

Altimeters measure elevation using barometric pressure. Really good electronic altimeters are highly accurate. The altimeters that come installed in bicycle computers are rarely fail-proof. Consequently, the readings from them can be inaccurate by plus or minus 200 feet. I have used the same Cateye computer throughout all the research to provide a consistency in the estimated elevations. That said, there were occasions when the read-out on the computer did not match published elevations. If the start of a ride had a known elevation I adjusted the altimeter to reflect this number. If, however, the start of a ride and the highest point on the ride had published elevations, I used only the first number and then used the spot elevations provided by the computer during the ride: I did not reset the altimeter to match the high elevation point. In most instances, the computer provided a high-point reading that closely matched the published elevation.

When completing these rides, you may find that your altimeter reading does not match mine. That's to be expected. The elevations provided in the trail descriptions are provided only as a guide. Treat them as such and they won't affect your riding pleasure.

Puget Sound

The stretch of saltwater that defines this area also squeezes its urban population into lands east, south, and north of the Seattle city limits. The city's hour-glass figure bordered on two sides by shimmering water looks great from the air. An aerial view also shows that there's a dearth of open space right next to town, and a watery edge to the west.

To get in a decent bike ride almost certainly requires a drive. (You could conceivably take your bike on a Metro bus to Tiger Mountain's north side.) The farther you are prepared to drive the quieter the trail will likely be when you reach it. Conversely, the trails closest to the urban fringe are inevitably the busiest (i.e., Tiger Mountain).

Several long-term projects have restored defunct railways into pleasing unpaved trails that combine easy grades with scenery and feats of railroad engineering. The potential to expand routes that tap into this long-distance spine is enormous, since the surrounding lands are often publicly owned. More and more energy will have to go into developing new trails to compensate for the riding areas that are lost due to development, particularly on the Eastside, Seattle's suburban fringe east of Lake Washington.

The area boasts a good selection of trails suited to beginners, as well as those for the more technically inclined riders. The latter include members of the Backcountry Bicycle Trails Club, who deserve praise for not only their advocacy position but for their willingness to put their backs into building and maintaining trails.

Rides included in this chapter are largely on public land ("public" in this instance ranges from city to state university ownership) that will likely continue to be made available to riders. One ride is on privately owned land (Victor Falls) that is open to public recreation, a situation that could potentially change should the land be sold or developed. All the rides in this chapter are within 75 minutes of Seattle on Interstate 5 or I-90.

Once you've ridden all these routes and would like to see more without driving farther, consider putting your energies into campaigning for renewed access to Cougar Regional Park (a decision by Metropolitan King County Council banned bikes) or pressing for entirely new trails. There are advocacy groups listed in the Appendix that would love to tap into your passion for more riding areas.

The Big Pack Loop

Location:	5 miles southwest of Eatonville, in the Charles L. Pack Experimental Forest.
Distance:	9.1-mile loop.
Tread:	Gravel logging roads, some singletrack.
Time:	2 to 3 hours.
Aerobic level:	Easy to moderate.
Technical difficulty:	1–2.
Best time to ride:	March to October.
Facilities:	Toilet and water available.
Land status:	Pack Experimental Forest, University of Washington.
Maps:	Small map produced by the University of Washington.
Access:	From Seattle, drive south on Interstate 5 for 26 miles to the Washington Route 161 exit (signed to Puyallup). Just before Puyallup, go east one mile on WA 167 and then turn south again on WA 161. Continue on WA 161 for 24 miles farther to Eatonville. Five miles beyond Eatonville, turn right onto WA 7. You'll see the entrance to the Pack Experimental Forest on the left just beyond this intersection.

NOTES ON THE TRAIL

Tooling around in the Pack Experimental Forest is like riding in a European park. Since it doesn't have millions of acres to look after, the University of Washington operates a high level of management and maintenance in its forest holding down Eatonville way. Since most of the trails are gated, you won't encounter many people breezing through in their four-wheel-drive vehicles. This adds to the park-like ambience. But don't go thinking this loop is a total picnic in the park. There are hills, mud, and obstacles to keep your mind busy. All of the foregoing makes this an ideal setting for beginners trying to hone their trail skills, or for families. If you go during the week, stop at the gatehouse for information on possible logging or research that may be taking place.

The Big Pack Loop

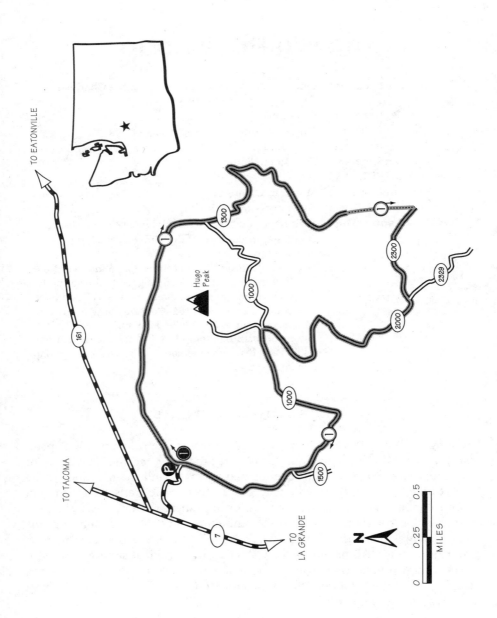

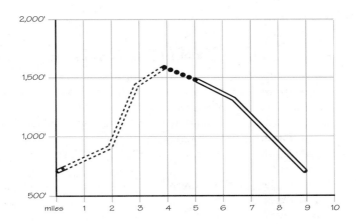

THE RIDE

0.0 At the parking lot next to the administration center on the corner of 453rd Street East, follow the signs for Murphy's Ranch.

0.2 Reach a gate across road 1000. Go under it onto the dirt/gravel road.

0.7 Road begins to climb. You'll shortly get view of Mt. Rainier.

1.9 Steel tanks. Keep right at the junction. Elevation 940 feet.

2.0 Junction. Go left on road 1300.

2.7 Road 1300 keeps climbing, now through a logged area.

3.0 Junction. Keep right on road 1300. Elevation 1,430 feet.

3.3 Junction. Keep straight on road 1300.

3.7 Watch for a blue diamond marker on tree on your left. This marks a short section of singletrack used by horses. It starts off smooth but is churned and rutted in the lower portion. Elevation 1,600 feet.

4.3 Turn right on road 2300.

5.3 Turn right on road 2000. You head uphill through an area that has been clear-cut. Elevation 1,455 feet.

5.9 Great views as you pass the cleared area.

6.5 Six-way junction. This is Kirkland Pass, elevation 1,380 feet. For the fun of it, follow the signs for Hugo Peak, climbing the short hill to reach 1,475 feet. I won't ruin the surprise of what you can see from the top. Turn around and pedal back to Kirkland Pass and follow road 1000 downhill. And quite a descent it is, too.

8.4 Junction with road 1500. Keep right.

9.0 Keep left at gate. Elevation 745 feet.

9.1 Back to the main parking lot. If you parked in the lower lot, continue following the road downhill.

Cranberry Lake

Location:	2 miles west of downtown Anacortes.
Distance:	5.2-mile loop.
Tread:	Predominantly singletrack, some doubletrack.
Time:	1.5 to 2 hours.
Aerobic level:	Moderate.
Technical difficulty:	2–4.
Best time to ride:	April to November.
Facilities:	None.
Land status:	Anacortes Community Forest Lands.
Maps:	Anacortes Community Forest Lands (available from Anacortes Cyclery).
Access:	From Seattle, drive north on Interstate 5. Go west on Washington Highway 20 toward Anacortes. Upon entering the city, turn right on Commercial Avenue, toward downtown. Drive 1.3 miles and turn left on WA 20 Spur, signed to the San Juan ferries. Follow it for 1.6 miles to Georgia Avenue (the seventh street) and turn left. As you climb uphill look for a sign on the right pointing to Cranberry Lake. Turn right on the dirt road and park at the top.

NOTES ON THE TRAIL

Once you've been to the Anacortes Community Forest Lands and have spun your wheels around Cranberry Lake, you'll agree that this is a ride to relish. This is especially true if you use this outing as an introduction to the wider opportunities these public lands offer, which include lakes once used for the city's water supply. One caveat about riding on the community forest lands: It is very easy to get lost. There are trails that wander off to the right and off to the left, trails that loop around, and some that even end up on private property. Since the Anacortes community has done such a stalwart job of stewarding this land over the years and maintaining access to a variety of users, visitors should be primed on where it's best to ride and not ride. Following this loop will keep within the confines of the forest and provide an experience that mixes short sections of technical terrain with tracts of easier stuff. This might be the perfect ride for a novice willing to test his or her root-hopping mettle. Many of the trails in the forest are signed, though the signing system looks like it was devised by a committee that couldn't reach a consensus.

Cranberry Lake

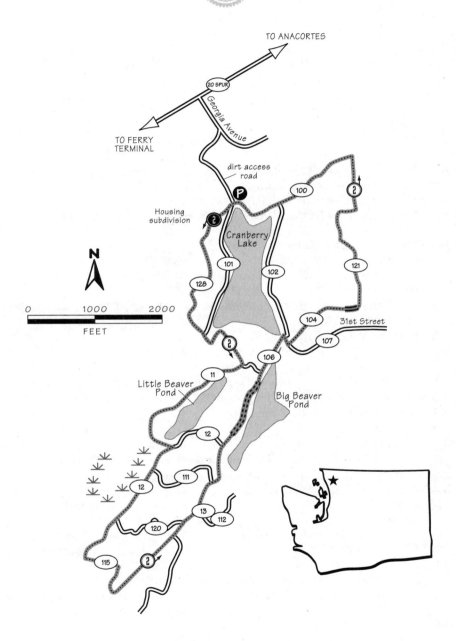

TO ANACORTES

20 SPUR

Georgia Avenue

TO FERRY
TERMINAL

dirt access
road

P

Housing
subdivision

2

100

2

Cranberry
Lake

101

102

121

128

104

31st Street

107

2

106

11

Little Beaver
Pond

Big Beaver
Pond

12

111

12

13

112

120

115

2

N

0   1000   2000
FEET

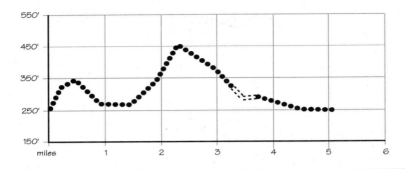

THE RIDE

0.0 Elevation 250 feet. With the lake on your right at the trailhead, ride up Trail 127 on the left. After a short steep section you'll shortly see homes through the trees and a junction with Trail 128. Go left.

0.2 The technical difficulty lessens after this section of roots and rocks. Elevation 315 feet.

0.5 Trail climbs again. Elevation 340 feet.

0.7 T-junction. Trail 128 ends. Go left. Elevation 295 feet.

0.8 Trail drops down toward the lake. Stay on main trail. 240 feet.

1.0 Junction with Trail 11. Go right. Elevation 265 feet.

1.2 Pass a tree on the right that announces the end of Trail 11 and start of Trail 109. Keep straight.

1.3 Junction with Trail 129. Go left. Elevation 280 feet.

1.5 Junction with Trail 110. Go left. The trail follows a wetland and you'll shortly cross a wooden bridge. Elevation 270 feet.

1.6 Junction with Trail 12. Take a sharp right on Trail 12. Elevation 275 feet.

1.9 Trail 12 becomes Trail 115. Stay on Trail 115 at its junction with Trail 120.

2.1 Downshift for a stiff little climb.

2.3 Hill tops out at 450 feet.

2.6 Start of tricky descent. Watch for loose stones and soil.

2.7 Trail 116 merges from the right. Continue downhill as Trail 115 becomes Trail 13.

2.9 T-junction with Trail 10. Elevation 285 feet. Go left.

3.4 Pass the end of Beaver Lake on a short section of jeep road. Trail 10 ends. Continue on Trail 106, which re-enters the woods on singletrack. Elevation 290 feet.

3.5 Cross stream on wooden bridge and follow Trail 101 to the right briefly. After a few yards alongside Cranberry Lake, turn uphill on Trail 107. Elevation 250 feet.

3.6 Junction with Trail 104. Go left. Elevation 295 feet.

3.8 A water tank is visible as you follow Trail 104. The trail splinters here: Take the path closest to the fence and turn right on the gravel road past the gate. Watch for Trail 121 leading into the woods opposite the Kingdom Hall.

3.9 Turn left on Trail 121.

4.4 Trail branches. Keep left and into the woods. (You can see homes on the right.) You'll shortly be climbing. Elevation 250 feet.

4.6 Turn left on Trail 100. Elevation rises to 285 feet and then drops back down to the lakeside.

5.2 Back to the trailhead.

Heart and Whistle Loop

Location:	2 miles south of Anacortes.
Distance:	9.9-mile loop.
Tread:	Dirt singletrack, some pavement.
Time:	2 to 2.5 hours.
Aerobic level:	Moderate.
Technical difficulty:	2–4.
Best time to ride:	May to October.
Facilities:	None.
Land status:	Anacortes Community Forest Lands.
Maps:	Anacortes Community Forest Lands (available from Anacortes Cyclery on Commercial Avenue).
Access:	From Seattle, drive north on Interstate 5. Go west on Washington Highway 20 toward Anacortes. Upon entering the city, turn left on Commercial Avenue. (This is the direction away from downtown.) Turn right on Fidalgo and then right on 41st. Follow it for one mile to A Avenue. Go right for 0.3 mile and park on the left, outside the yellow gated entrance to the Anacortes Community Forest Lands.

NOTES ON THE TRAIL

There are so many trails and quiet roads in the Anacortes Community Forest Lands that an enterprising rider could create dozens of loops. Here's the one yours truly came up with, though I make no claim to originality. It's a blend of exciting downhills, technical uphill, and just plain fun. And since the area is laced with trails that are not always signed, expect some orienteering, too.

THE RIDE

0.0 From the entrance on A Avenue (which becomes Havekost Road) ride south away from town. Elevation 255 feet.

0.5 Turn left into a development called Parkside and take the first right, Hickory Avenue.

0.7 Just after the first set of mailboxes, turn right on a short, unpaved service road. You'll see a sewer cover at the end, as well as a trail that leads into the woods. The trail goes around the rear of some houses and heads east. Elevation 360 feet.

Heart and Whistle Loop

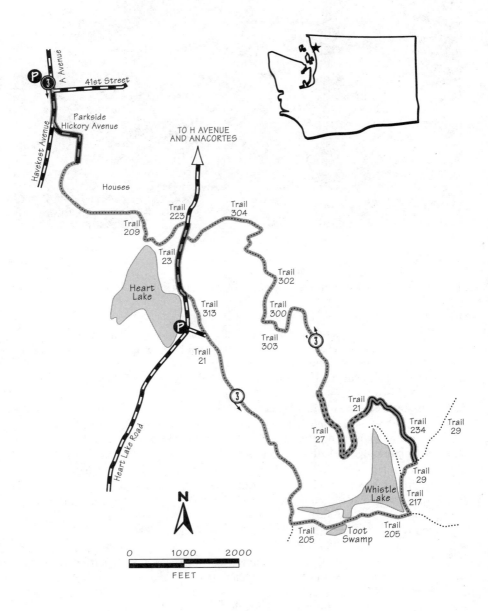

A Avenue

P 3

41st Street

Parkside
Hickory Avenue

Havekost Avenue

TO H AVENUE
AND ANACORTES

Houses

Trail
223

Trail
304

Trail
209

Trail
23

Heart
Lake

Trail
302

Trail
313

Trail
300

P

Trail
303

3

Trail
21

3

Trail
21

Trail
234

Trail
29

Trail
27

Trail
29

Whistle
Lake

Trail
217

Heart Lake Road

N

Trail
205

Toot
Swamp

Trail
205

0   1000   2000

FEET

Low clearance on the Heart and Whistle Loop.

1.0 At the first junction, go left.

1.2 Turn right at the next intersection. (You'll pass a trail that approaches from the left. Ignore it.)

1.3 Turn right at the next intersection.

1.4 Turn left at the next intersection and then take an immediate right.

1.5 Turn right at the next intersection. Just beyond this intersection you'll cross a creek bed and go uphill briefly. Keep right.

1.6 Heart Lake Road. Turn right on the paved road and proceed briefly uphill and then downhill.

2.3 Pass the entrance to Heart Lake State Park.

2.4 Look for a flaking white gate set slightly back from the road on the left. Turn here and go around gate. In 50 feet, turn right and begin to climb.

2.8 Keep climbing. Elevation 510 feet.

3.0 At the top of this climb you'll see a big rock. Go left. Elevation 660 feet.

3.3 Begin a descent, which becomes quite steep. Elevation 640 feet.

3.7 A sign at this intersection offers two routes to Whistle Lake. Go right on Trail 205. Elevation 565 feet.

4.0 Follow the sign for Trail 205. Go left. Elevation 500 feet.

4.1 Ascend briefly to 530 feet.

4.2 You'll glimpse a body of water known as Toot Swamp. Keep left on Trail 205.

4.3 The terrain becomes ever more challenging to ride as you approach the lake. Elevation 475 feet.

4.4 Keep right and scramble up the rocky trail.

4.8 Where a collapsed Douglas-fir is perched six feet off the trail, turn left back toward the lake.

4.9 You're now riding alongside the lake. Elevation 495 feet.

5.1 Trail 205 is closed to mountain bikes at this junction. Turn right and look for a sign that says Trail 29, and follow it away from the lake.

5.2 Just before a short gravel section (a repair to a muddy area), look for a trail on the left. This is Trail 234.

5.8 Go left. Just beyond the junction you'll see a service road. There's a pit toilet here and to the left of it, a trail (21) heading uphill. Take it. Elevation 490 feet.

6.2 Go right on Trail 27. (In August 1998 there was a pile of gravel at the intersection.)

7.1 After a short but exhilarating section, the trail turns left and back into the woods proper. Elevation 720 feet.

7.2 Go right at trail junction. Trail begins a descent here.

7.8 You'll see a white corral fence in the distance. At intersection, go left. Elevation 370 feet.

7.9 Go left. Keep on this main trail, ignoring the numerous spurs.

8.3 Keep right.

8.4 In quick succession, take a right, then a left, and then another right.

8.5 Cross Heart Lake Road and follow Trail 211. In a few yards you'll see a sign for Trail 223. Go left on it, and take a left at the following junction.

8.8 Take a right on Trail 209.

8.9 Go left at next intersection. Elevation 385 feet. You're now within sight of houses. Take another left.

9.0 Go right (toward the houses) and then immediately left. You're now riding behind the houses.

9.3 Exit the woodsy trail at the service road next to the sewer cover.

9.4 Proceed up the gravel and grass road until you reach pavement. Turn left, then take a right onto Havekost Road.

9.9 Return to your parked vehicle.

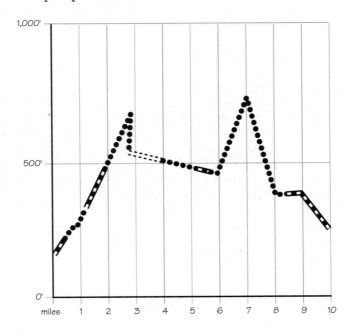

Iron Horse State Park

Location:	Hyak, Snoqualmie Pass.
Distance:	66 miles, out and back.
Tread:	Rail-trail with packed gravel, packed dirt, and loose gravel in places.
Time:	4 to 5 hours.
Aerobic level:	Easy.
Technical difficulty:	1.
Best time to ride:	April to October.
Facilities:	Vault toilet at trailhead; camping options nearby at state and Forest Service campgrounds.
Land status:	Washington State Parks & Recreation Commission.
Maps:	Green Trails Snoqualmie Pass.
Access:	From Seattle, take Interstate 90 east to Exit 54 (Hyak). At the off-ramp turn right and then take an immediate left, following signs for Iron Horse State Park. Drive down this access road and turn right before reaching a highway maintenance depot. Follow this road for another 0.5 mile and park in the Keechelus Trailhead lot. You must display a Forest Service trailhead parking permit in your vehicle. (For more information on these parking passes, see page 6).

NOTES ON THE TRAIL

Marvel at the engineering feats of the Milwaukee, Chicago, St. Paul, and Pacific Railroad while enjoying gentle grades that take you up and through Snoqualmie Pass. The undoubted highlight of this ride is the always dark and usually dripping 2.3-mile-long Snoqualmie Tunnel. Better than any ride dreamed up by Disney, the tunnel will either spook or excite you. Strap on a light because this is a shade blacker than pitch. When finally you pop out into the kleig lights of daytime you're in for a long, slow descent of 1,000 feet with wide views of the valley shared by the interstate. To keep things interesting you'll cross a couple of high trestles and pass under a reconstructed snowshed. Choo-choo sounds are optional. You can customize this ride by turning around sooner.

Note: In some areas, the trail is identified on road signs as the John Wayne Pioneer Trail.

Iron Horse State Park

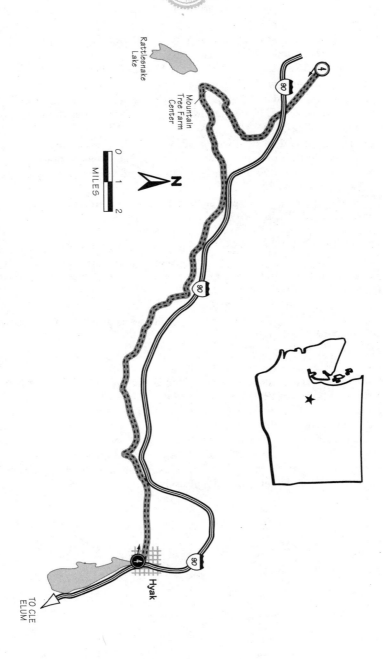

0.0 From the Keechelus Trailhead, turn right toward the tunnel. Elevation 2,945 feet.

0.6 Proceed past the gate.

0.8 Don your jacket, test your headlamp for the dark and drippy ride through the Snoqualmie Tunnel.

3.1 Hit by blinding daylight as you emerge from the dank interior.

3.9 Pass over Olallie Creek. Elevation 2,880 feet.

5.1 Rock slide and avalanche area. You can see remnants of the huge snowshed that was demolished in the summer of 1998. Ride under the remaining (and now restored) section.

7.8 An elegant curved trestle sweeps across a stream more than a hundred feet below. Be careful on the loose red gravel, and stay away from the edges.

12.4 Cross Alice Creek. You continue to descend down the valley around curves and straightaways.

13.4 The railroad cut through rock to round this corner. To your right is a bend in the Snoqualmie River.

14.4 Elevation 1,975 feet.

16.3 Hall Creek trestle. This magnificent bridge over Hall Creek was damaged in a landslide during the eighties but has now been restored by Washington State Parks. Eventually, all bridges will have sturdy fenced edges like this one.

17.8 Change Creek. Elevation 1,785 feet.

19.4 Twin Falls (exit to I-90 and trailhead). Elevation 1,470 feet.

20.9 Elevation 1,535 feet. Beyond here the trail moves away from the freeway and is considerably less noisy.

21.9 Elevation 1,465 feet.

22.9 Boxley Creek. Elevation 1,400 feet.

23.9 Rattlesnake Lake Recreation Area. This is the official end of the Iron Horse State Park Trail. In the summer, you'll see cars parked in the lots next to the lake. Follow the trail downhill until you reach the paved road. Turn right and ride on the road until you see a trail on your immediate right where there is a pedestrian crossing. You can also start or finish your ride here.

24.9 Turn right back onto the trail and follow it as it parallels the paved road. You'll shortly see a King County Parks Department sign announcing the Snoqualmie Valley Trail, which you can follow into North Bend and beyond.

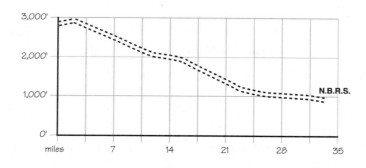

27.2 Reach another restored wooden trestle. Elevation 1,035 feet.

28.5 Elevation 1,000 feet.

30.3 Cross the South Fork of the Snoqualmie River. Elevation 720 feet.

30.5 Cross under I-90 and follow the trail across busy SE Tanner Road. There's a plaque on the right next to the river that provides historical information. Continue on the trail as it cross several minor roads.

33.0 This is the site of the former North Bend depot, long since demolished. Elevation 520 feet.

Iron Horse State Park
(East-bound)

Location:	Hyak, Snoqualmie Pass.
Distance:	12 miles, out and back.
Tread:	Rail-trail with packed and loose gravel.
Time:	1 to 2 hours.
Aerobic level:	Easy.
Technical difficulty:	1.
Best time to ride:	April to October.
Facilities:	Vault toilet at trailhead.
Land status:	Washington State Parks and Recreation Commission.
Maps:	Green Trails Snoqualmie Pass.
Access:	From Seattle, drive east on Interstate 90 to exit 54 (Hyak). Go right and then take an immediate left, following signs for Iron Horse State Park. Drive down this access road and turn right before reaching a highway maintenance depot. Follow this road for another 0.5 mile and park in the Keechelus Trailhead lot.

NOTES ON THE TRAIL

Mountain-bike rides hardly come easier than this. Not bad scenery, either. The lake (the stumps around the shoreline reveal its creation as a reservoir) adds a bit of interest, as do the forest and the old railway route.

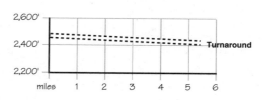

Not a spectacular ride, but it has many attributes that make it a popular outing for families seeking a car-free environment. You can also combine this with the Spillway Loop, or keep heading east toward Cle Elum for an additional 20 miles of riding.

THE RIDE

0.0 Trailhead parking lot. Go left.
0.5 Pass gate blocking motor vehicles.

Iron Horse State Park (East-bound)

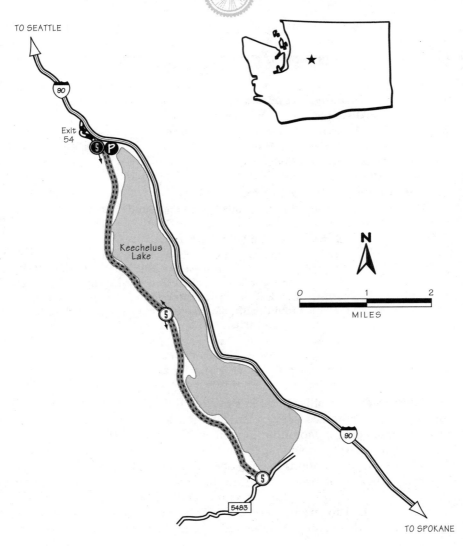

1.9 Stream crossing.

2.5 Concrete wall on your right is all that remains of a former railway snowshed. Sound from I-90 is audible across the lake here.

3.0 Trail cuts through rocky area.

4.5 Trail crosses unguarded bridge. Keep to the middle.

6.0 Cross a steel bridge and reach the gate at Forest Road 5483. Turn around here or ride the Spillway Loop (Ride 9, page 46) for an additional 5.8 miles of easy biking.

12.0 Return to trailhead.

Lost Valley Loop

Location:	12 miles west of Olympia, in the Capitol State Forest.
Distance:	14.1-mile loop.
Tread:	Gravel roads, dirt singletrack.
Time:	4 to 5 hours.
Aerobic level:	Moderate.
Technical difficulty:	2–3.
Best time to ride:	May to October.
Facilities:	Primitive toilets at campground; water.
Land status:	DNR South Puget Sound.
Maps:	DNR Capitol State Forest.
Access:	From Seattle (or Olympia), drive south on Interstate 5 to exit 95. Head west to and through Littlerock. Not quite a mile beyond Littlerock, turn right on Waddell Creek Road. Proceed for approximately 3.1 miles until the Middle Waddell campground. Park in the day-use area.

NOTES ON THE TRAIL

The Capitol State Forest is Olympia's playground. It's a place where people come to hike, ride horses, camp, picnic, target shoot, cruise off-road motorcycles, and, of course, pilot mountain bikes. Not all the uses are compatible but, that said, there's enough space in the forest to have your own adventure. The forest also contains logging operations, which result in the relocation or destruction of trails from time to time. Once you've gained your bearings (a DNR map is highly recommended; Thurston County Sheriff's deputies have had to rescue people lost in the forest), you'll find lots to discover within this managed woodland—singletrack, hills, natural hazards,

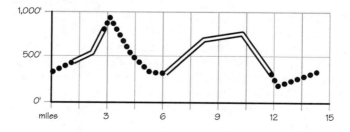

Lost Valley Loop

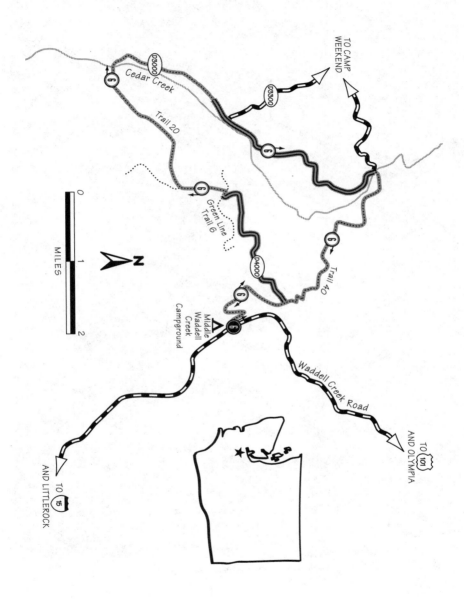

This bridge is part of recent trail improvements in the Capitol State Forest.

wildlife, and interesting scenery. Be sure to follow the instructions carefully as many trails and most roads are not marked.

THE RIDE

0.0 Standing with your back to the entrance gate to the campground, go right on the second trail from the gate. You parallel the road briefly.

0.6 Road D-4000, which is paved initially. Go left.

1.1 Road, now gravel, starts to climb.

2.3 Elevation 650 feet. There are numerous roads that come in from each side. Ignore these and stay on this main forest road.

2.9 Just beyond another intersection, you'll see a trail crossing the road you're on. Turn right onto the trail. (A sign says closed to motorized vehicles.) This is Green Line Trail 6.

3.2 Reach the intersection with Trail 20. Elevation 985 feet. Go left.

3.5 Transition from mature forest to an area overgrown with alder, ferns, and Scotchbroom.

3.6 Cross a partially collapsed bridge. Watch out for roots on the trail, as well as evidence of equine visits.

3.7 Keep right, ignoring trail leading off to the left.

5.2 Bump and steer your way down the Lost Valley until you reach Cedar Creek. Ford the creek and turn right on road D-3000, which parallels the creek for a couple of miles.

7.5 Pass an open area that was logged in 1998.

8.2 Junction for Camp Weekend. Keep on D-3000. Elevation 710 feet.

8.3 Ignoring the gated road on the left, keep right.

8.6 Just beyond gated road, look for trail on the right. Turn right onto this trail.

9.4 Keep right at fork in trail. Watch for badly rutted section.

9.9 Cross gravel road.

10.4 Cross another gravel road. Elevation 795 feet.

10.5 Trail forks, keep right.

11.4 Trail crossroads. Keep straight and prepare for a tricky chute-like descent.

12.2 Trail junction. Keep right. Elevation 110 feet.

12.7 Cross bridge.

13.1 Trail junction. Keep right.

13.2 Cross a red metal bridge and keep straight ahead (uphill) for campground.

13.5 Ride alongside rail fence until large parking lot. If you didn't park here, head toward the exit and turn left on a trail that parallels the road.

14.1 Return to main entrance and your vehicle.

Skookum-White River

Location:	6 miles east of Greenwater in the Mount Baker-Snoqualmie National Forest.
Distance:	12-mile loop.
Tread:	Singletrack, gravel and dirt roads, some pavement.
Time:	4.5 to 5.5 hours.
Aerobic level:	Easy.
Technical difficulty:	3–4.
Best time to ride:	May to October.
Facilities:	None.
Land status:	Mount Baker-Snoqualmie National Forest, White River Ranger District.
Maps:	Mount Baker-Snoqualmie National Forest, White River Ranger District; Green Trails Greenwater.
Access:	From Seattle, go south on Interstate 5 and turn east on Washington Route 18 to Auburn. Then drive south on WA 167 and then WA 410, sign-posted to Mount Rainier. You'll pass through Enumclaw and then the small settlement of Greenwater. Six miles beyond Greenwater watch for a scenic overlook and about a half-mile beyond it, Forest Road 73. Turn right and cross the bridge. You'll see a small parking lot on the right opposite the trailhead.

NOTES ON THE TRAIL

The mineral-rich White River is a near-constant companion on this highly varied and, at times, challenging loop that combines parts of the Skookum Flats and White River Trails. Skookum Flats is that rare breed of trail that is technical in places but never rises very high or gets especially steep for extended distances. But as you slog up a slippery slope or two, picture the blissful forest trail on the other side of the river. Skookum Flats is the boiled cabbage part of this ride meal; the White River Trail is chocolate mousse. First, you have to eat your vegetables. And that means negotiating lots of roots, loose slopes, rocks, and, depending on the time of year, puddles. There are also drop-offs where there's nothing but air between you and the river. This ride is certainly no secret. It can be busy on weekends, with other riders as well as hikers.

Skookum—White River

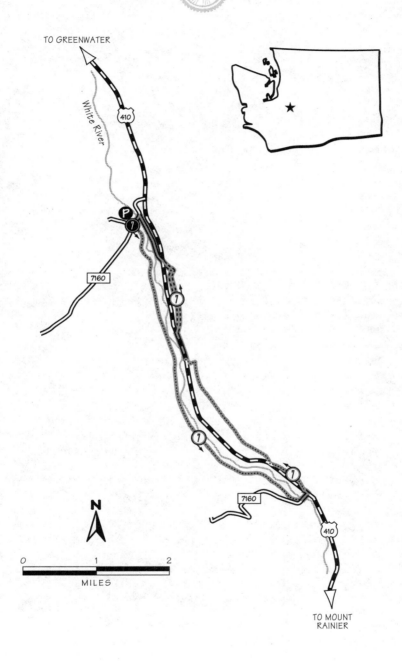

TO GREENWATER

White River

410

P

7160

N

0   1   2
MILES

7160

410

TO MOUNT
RAINIER

Some riders are convinced that Skookum means twisting and turning.
PHOTO BY JAY ROBERTSON.

THE RIDE

0.0 Head up through old-growth forest from the trailhead. Elevation 2,105 feet.

1.0 This is like the woods of a fairy tale, tall and benign. So peaceful. Some ups and downs. Elevation 2,180 feet.

1.7 First of numerous rocky sections. Elevation 2,225 feet.

2.2 A huge blown cedar straddles the air above the trail. More technical challenges await.

3.0 Still technical in places but much easier.

4.0 More small tricky sections. Elevation 2,380 feet.

4.1 Trail climbs steeply on a slope with obstacles. Drop-off on one side.

4.5 Uphill smooth section. Elevation 2,530 feet.

4.7 Downhill to the river and junction with narrow suspension bridge. Elevation 2,400 feet. Stay on west side of the river.

4.8 After a brief climb, descend to the river bank.

5.1 Cross a rough-log bridge and then climb up through a mixed forest of young and older trees.

5.6 Ride along wide ledge above the river. Enough light gets through here for a healthy groundmass of salal. Trail is relatively flat now.

5.8 Trail splits. Keep left.

6.0 Junction. A misleading sign indicates that the Mount Rainier National Park boundary is 2.5 miles away. Ignore the sign and go right.

6.1 Reach FR 7160. Turn left and cross the high bridge. Turn left onto the shoulder of WA 410. Ride down the highway for about 100 yards. Look for a trail sign on the slope to the right of the road.

6.3 After riding up the slope you'll see a sign for the White River Trail 1199. Go left in the direction of Camp Sheppard down a nice, smooth trail. Elevation 2,485 feet.

6.8 This trail is in such contrast to the Skookum Flats Trail.

7.2 Keep rolling, dipping, and rising through a pristine forest. Elevation 2,535 feet. At the junction, keep right.

7.8 More ups and downs, but easy stuff with a few roots and ruts thrown in. Keep right on the White River Trail. If you want to look at the Snoquera Falls, take the sharp right trail heading uphill. Elevation 2,470 feet.

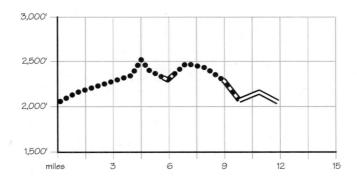

7.9 Keep right at junction. If you end up on a dirt road, double back. The road leads to Camp Sheppard. The trail becomes a little indistinct here because of a washout.

8.1 Cross the first of three clearings. Elevation 2,435 feet.

8.6 Junction. Keep straight and ignore the multitude of signs. Elevation 2,390 feet.

9.0 Junction. Keep right.

9.2 Drop down steeply to WA 410 and turn right back toward Greenwater. Elevation 2,270 feet.

9.9 Turn right on FR. 7150, the first gravel road leading off the highway. Climb up briefly and ride past a series of vacation cabins.

11.0 Descend to the highway again and cross over to The Dalles Campground. Elevation 2,170 feet. Once beyond the campground entrance, turn right and follow the paved service road all the way to where it turns.

11.4 Go straight, stopping to ogle at the 500-year-old Douglas-fir on your right. Follow the trail leading away from the campground. Elevation 2,125 feet.

12.0 After a short climb you emerge at FR 73. Turn left and cross the bridge.

Snoqualmie Valley Trail

Location:	Old railroad 2 miles south of Duvall.
Distance:	16.9 miles, one way.
Tread:	Packed gravel and packed dirt rail-trail.
Time:	1.5 to 2.5 hours (one way).
Aerobic level:	Easy. This old railroad grade was built for lumbering steam locomotives.
Technical difficulty:	1.
Best time to ride:	Year-round.
Facilities:	None at trailhead; towns of Carnation and Duvall have food and toilets.
Land status:	King County.
Maps:	King County Bicycling Guide and map.
Access:	From Seattle, take Washington Route 520 east to Interstate 405. Go north to exit 23, signed for WA 522 Woodinville and Monroe. After 1 mile, go east on the Woodinville-Duvall Road. Proceed for 8.5 miles to Duvall. Turn right onto WA 203 toward Fall City. Drive just over 2 miles beyond Duvall to the intersection with NE 124th Street. Park in the gravel area on the left.

NOTES ON THE TRAIL

A wonderful place to introduce beginners to the joys of off-roading. King County purchased the former Everett branch of the Milwaukee, Chicago, St. Paul, and Pacific right-of-way through the farmlands of the Snoqualmie Valley when the railroad abandoned the line. Eventually this trail will hook up with several other rail-trails. You can tackle the trail in sections, or ride it

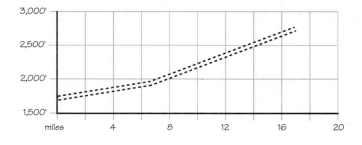

Snoqualmie Valley Trail

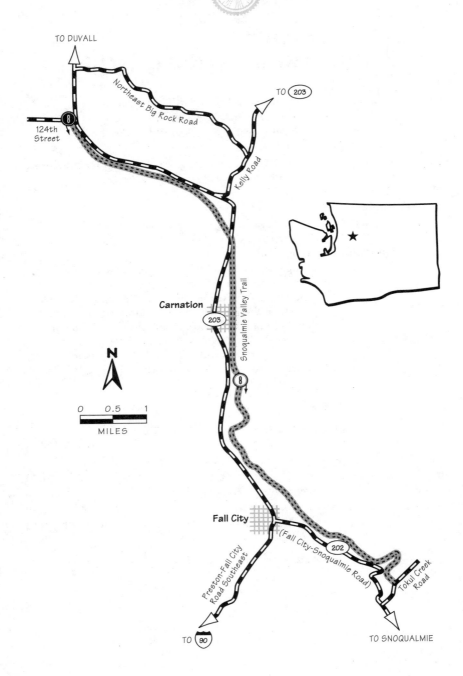

TO DUVALL

Northeast Big Rock Road

TO 203

124th Street

8

Kelly Road

Carnation

203

Snoqualmie Valley Trail

N

0   0.5   1

MILES

8

Fall City

(Fall City-Snoqualmie Road)

202

Preston-Fall City Road Southeast

Tokul Creek Road

TO 90

TO SNOQUALMIE

almost the entire way to the scenic Snoqualmie Falls, enjoying views from restored high trestles as the trail climbs up the valley. The mileages in parentheses apply if you start the ride in Carnation, rather than outside Duvall.

THE RIDE

0.0   Cross the Duvall-Fall City Road and turn left on the trail (look for the gate).

0.2   Doubletrack leads to an unrenovated trestle. Walk your bike across the big beams.

0.4   Second unimproved trestle. Walk your bike across.

1.9   First improved trestle. Glide right over it and the meandering Snoqualmie River below.

3.1   Pass a trail parking lot.

3.5   Wetlands with lots of cattails on the left.

3.8   Pass another trail parking lot.

4.7   Trail is open to fields on both sides.

5.2   Trail crosses Duvall-Fall City Road. Watch for fast-moving traffic.

6.6 (0.0)   Nick Loutsis Park, Entwistle Street, Carnation. Turn right here for services in town.

7.1 (0.5)   Cross the broad Tolt River on a nicely rebuilt bridge.

7.2 (0.6)   Berringer berry farm on the left.

7.8 (1.2)   Cross a paved road.

8.9 (2.3)   First high viaduct. Look for grazing horses below. Trail transitions from gravel to packed dirt.

9.6 (3.0)   Notice how the trail is now much higher than the valley floor.

11.1 (4.5)   Area restored from earlier landslide. Metal shoring visible on the "drop" side of the trail.

11.3 (4.7)   Another trestle.

13.5 (6.9)   New bridge replaces earlier trestle lost in a landslide.

13.7 (7.1)   Look for AT&T transcontinental cable relay station on the left.

13.7 (7.1)   Cross 356th Drive SE. One rail remains embedded in the pavement.

15.5 (8.9)   Loose gravel on trail.

15.6 (9.0)   Views to the south and west show converging sides of the valley.

16.0 (9.4)   Spectacular curved trestle.

16.9 (10.3)   Reach rebuilt tunnel below Tokul Creek Road. (Tunnel tends to contain broken glass.)

Note: To round out the ride, proceed through the tunnel for another 0.2 mile on the narrow trail and take the first left. This takes you to Tokul Creek Road. Turn left on it and ride about three-quarters of a mile downhill to the Snoqualmie Falls and Salish Lodge.

Spillway Loop

Location:	5 miles northwest of Easton, near Snoqualmie Pass.
Distance:	5.8-mile loop.
Tread:	Packed dirt, gravel road; some singletrack.
Time:	1 to 1.5 hours.
Aerobic level:	Moderate.
Technical difficulty:	1.
Best time to ride:	May to October.
Facilities:	Vault toilet and water at Crystal Springs Campground.
Land status:	Wenatchee National Forest, Cle Elum Ranger Station.
Maps:	Green Trails Snoqualmie Pass; Wenatchee National Forest.
Access:	From Seattle, drive east on Interstate 90 to exit 62. Go right for 1 mile to Crystal Springs Campground. Day fee or trailhead parking decal required.

NOTES ON THE TRAIL

A great beginners', kids', or warm-up loop that will put you right in the mood for further pedaling. It has all the essential ingredients—singletrack, creek crossings, whoop-de-woos, and very little climbing. It's pure fun.

THE RIDE

0.0 Start at Crystal Springs Campground and turn right, crossing the Yakima River.

0.9 Turn right onto Iron Horse State Park Trail.

2.5 The end of this trail section. Go right on FR 5480 briefly and then go behind the orange gate now facing you. You'll see the lake in the near distance. Evening sunlight enhances the ride as you head along the spillway berm. Elevation 2,517 feet.

3.7 End of spillway, keep right.

3.9 Go right at road junction.

4.1 At the sign "Authorized Vehicles Only Beyond This Point," take the rough track on the left.

4.3 Track veers to the right.

4.4 Keep right. The electric utility poles go straight, you don't.

4.6 Cross the first of three pole bridges. If you're a novice, you'll want to walk.

Spillway Loop

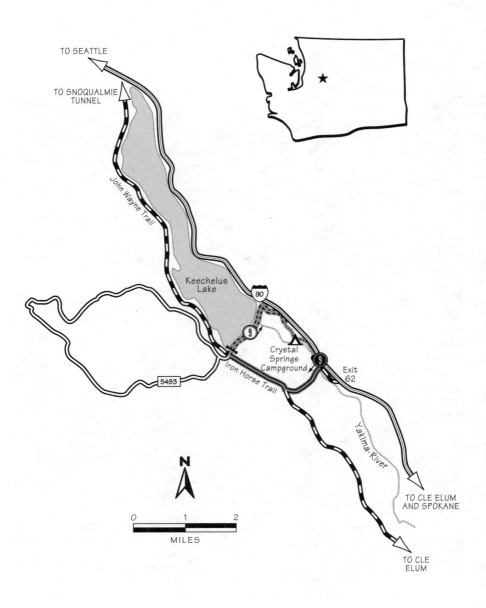

TO SEATTLE

TO SNOQUALMIE
TUNNEL

John Wayne Trail

Keechelus
Lake

90

9

Crystal
Springs
Campground

9

Exit
62

Iron Horse Trail

5483

Yakima River

TO CLE ELUM
AND SPOKANE

TO CLE
ELUM

N

0   1   2

MILES

By mid-summer there are lots of stumps visible in Keechelus Lake.

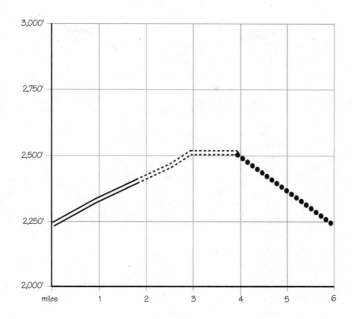

4.8 Keep right at junction.

5.2 As you wander through the woods, it's hard to believe the interstate is so close. Keep right and ride toward the log pile. You'll see another pole bridge just beyond. Cross it.

5.4 Cross last pole bridge.

5.8 After a final section that can be muddy, the trail ends next to site 21 at Crystal Springs Campground.

Preston Railroad & Northwest Timber Loop

Location:	Tiger Mountain State Forest, 5 miles southeast of Issaquah.
Distance:	11.5-mile loop.
Tread:	Packed gravel road, singletrack.
Time:	1.5 to 2 hours.
Aerobic level:	Mildly strenuous.
Technical difficulty:	3. Roots, rocks, other obstacles.
Best time to ride:	Trails closed October 15 to April 15.
Facilities:	Vault toilet.
Land status:	DNR, South Puget Sound Region.
Maps:	DNR Tiger Mountain State Forest.
Access:	From Seattle, take Interstate 90 east toward North Bend. Take exit 25 and go west 4 miles on Washington Route 18. Just past a sign announcing the Tiger Summit, look for the trailhead parking lot on the right.

Notes on the Trail

A good place to blow away the travails of the city with a vigorous uphill climb of more than 1,000 feet followed by some highly satisfying, if bumpy, downhill singletrack. This is among the closest singletrack to Seattle and can attract lots of weekend riders; midweek and evenings are less crowded. As you pound your way up the logging road (watch for trucks) to the true tread you get a sampling of views over "Pugetopolis" to the west. You'll want to stop and catch your breath after the 3.2-mile gravel ride. When finally you enter the Preston Railroad Trail, give thanks to the volunteers who built and maintain it.

The Ride

0.0 Both rides behind the parking lot are gated. Take the gravel road on the right and proceed uphill. Elevation 1,250 feet.

0.2 Pass the sign for the Northwest Timber Trail. This is where you'll exit back to the road.

Preston Railroad & Northwest Timber Loop

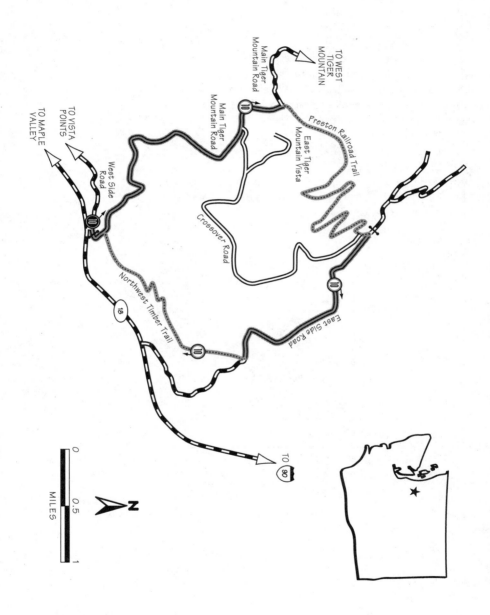

TO WEST TIGER MOUNTAIN

Main Tiger Mountain Road

Main Tiger Mountain Road

Main Tiger Mountain Road

Preston Railroad Trail

East Tiger Mountain Vista

TO VISTA POINTS

TO MAPLE VALLEY

West Side Road

Crossover Road

Northwest Timber Trail

East Side Road

18

TO 90

N

MILES

0   0.5   1

1.4   Viewpoint at 1,965 feet.

2.7   Junction with Crossover Road 5500. Keep left.

3.2   Entrance to Preston Railroad Trail (elevation 2,420). Turn right.

3.4   Trail climbs briefly through sparse second-growth forest.

3.7   Trail turns onto original railroad grade.

4.0   Rough terrain with lots of roots.

4.5   Trail turns back on itself.

5.5   More switchbacks.

6.1   Section with rocks, roots, and goo.

6.5   Trail begins to smooth out again.

6.9   End of Preston Railroad Trail (elevation 1,415). Turn left.

7.0   Keep right and follow gravel road downhill.

8.9   Turn right onto Northwest Timber Trail. Elevation 1,290.

9.2   Climb gently through open forest with lush green undergrowth.

9.8   Begin the descent. You can hear traffic on nearby roads.

10.0 Cross the first bridge.

10.6 Continue descending but with occasional short climbs.

11.3 Exit onto the Tiger Main Road. Go left.

11.5 Return to parking lot.

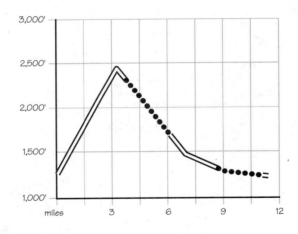

Victor Falls—Getting Acquainted

Location:	5 miles southeast of Bonny Lake.
Distance:	8.3-mile loop.
Tread:	Singletrack, jeep road, gravel road.
Time:	2 to 2.5 hours.
Aerobic level:	Moderate.
Technical difficulty:	2–3.
Best time to ride:	Year-round.
Facilities:	None.
Maps:	Victor Falls by Fer-Thur Directions Mapping Company available from Tacoma-area bike shops.
Land status:	Cascadia Corporation, which permits non-motorized visitors.
Access:	From Seattle, drive south on Interstate 5 to exit 149 for Washinton Route 516. Go east on WA 516 until the intersection with WA 167 (The Valley Freeway). Go south on it toward Puyallup and take the exit for WA 410 toward Mount Rainier. Drive east on WA 410 past Sumner and uphill to the light at the junction with the Old Buckley Highway within the city of Bonny Lake. Turn left at the light (you'll see two gas stations) and follow the Old Buckley Highway through Bonny Lake for 1.5 miles. At the foot of a hill, turn right on Angeline Road and head south (and under WA 410) until Rhodes Lake Road. Turn left, passing a sign advertising "Victor Falls Residential Estate." Proceed uphill past Victor Falls Elementary School and a series of subdivisions, where Rhodes Lake becomes 198th Street. Just over two miles from the Victor Falls sign is 131st Street and sign for Hillside Farms Christmas Trees. Park here in the small lot.

NOTES ON THE TRAIL

If ever an area should be snapped up and dedicated to mountain biking, it is
Victor Falls. The area was extensively logged in recent years, creating a
lattice of access roads that mountain bikers have liberally extended with a

Victor Falls

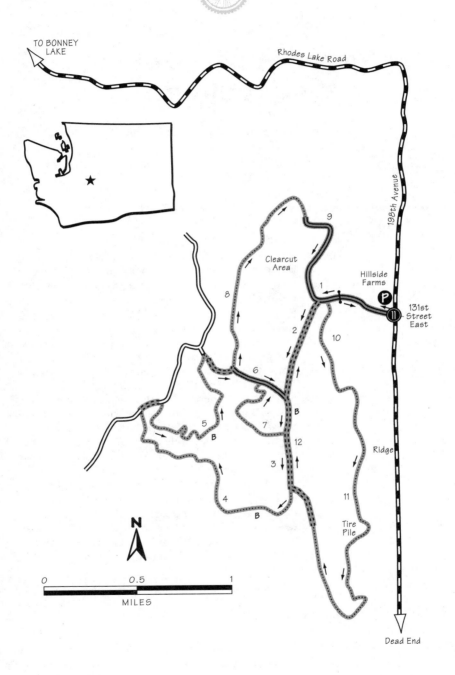

TO BONNEY LAKE

Rhodes Lake Road

Clearcut Area

Hillside Farms

131st Street East

198th Avenue

9

1

8

2

10

6

B

5

B

7

12

3

4

B

11

Ridge

Tire Pile

Dead End

N

0   0.5   1

MILES

series of singletrack trails. The area sits high above the glacier-carved Carbon River Valley and within squinting distance of the state's most distinctive landmark— Mount Rainier. You could not invent better terrain as a place to sample and test mountain bikes. There are hills and forests, ridges and plains. Largely because of the logging activities, and the proximity of more enticing trails within Mount Rainier National Park, there's nary

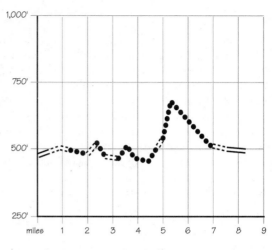

a hiker. You might come across the occasional equestrian but never a powered vehicle. There are some downsides to this nirvana—when it rains roads and trails flood in some places. But maybe you like a good shot of mud in the eye. A bigger drawback is, ironically, its size and number of trails. They are largely unmarked and can easily have you riding in circles. This introductory ride is designed to get you acquainted with the area and maybe just stop you from getting lost. Master it, then branch out on your own. And do buy one of the maps created by Jim Hendricks. It's indispensable. Puyallup Valley Mountain Bikers and Single Track Mind clubs hold regular, organized rides in this area. See Appendix for how to contact those clubs.

THE RIDE

0.0 From the parking lot head up the gravel road away from the paved road. Elevation 475 feet.

0.2 Pass behind gate and keep straight ahead on the access road. Elevation 510 feet.

0.5 Junction. Keep left, following the blue diamond marked "B." Elevation 480 feet.

1.0 Stay on the main access road.

2.0 T-junction. Take a right; continue to follow the route marked "B."

2.1 Watch for "B" sign and take a right into the woods on the singletrack trail. Elevation 480 feet.

2.3 Lots of twists, turns, roots, and dips to negotiate. Climbs a bit, too. Elevation 510 feet.

2.5 Three-way junction. Go right. Look for the "B" on a tree. Elevation 475 feet.

2.9 Junction. Go right, following "B." You have now completed the first loop. This part should look familiar. Proceed back down the access road you've previously ridden.

3.2 Turn right onto singletrack trail leading uphill into the woods.

3.5 More roots and ruts to tackle as you wind through the skinny trees. Elevation 500 feet.

3.7 Junction. Go left. Again, you've been here before. In about 100 feet, take the first right onto a wide and smooth singletrack.

3.9 Trail crossroads. Keep straight. Elevation 470 feet.

4.1 Trail crossroads. Keep straight.

4.2 Trail forks. Go left and back onto a more rugged trail. In another 100 yards or so, stay left again. Elevation 460 feet.

4.4 Reach the edge of a clear-cut area. You'll see homes on the left and, possibly, Rhodes Lake. Descend down through the logged land. Elevation 435 feet.

4.5 At junction, go right and proceed uphill on the rough logging road. Elevation 420 feet.

4.8 Reach junction near the main entrance gate where you came in. This time go straight across onto the uphill singletrack. Elevation 505 feet.

5.0 Go left at first fork in the trail. Downshift for some serious climbing. Elevation 545 feet.

5.2 You've now ridden up to the ridge. You follow it for a mile or so and then descend. Elevation 695 feet.

5.3 Trail crossroads. Keep straight. Elevation 690 feet.

5.8 Junction. Go left. Elevation 640 feet.

5.9 Go right. You'll see a pile of dumped tires in the woods just beyond the corner. Ride past the tires. Elevation 625 feet.

6.4 Junction. Go right. You'll see the paved road to the left. Elevation 585 feet.

6.9 Plunge downhill into what may be the least disturbed natural area. If it has been raining, this is where the puddles get seriously large. Elevation 520 feet.

7.1 Junction with access road. Yes, the selfsame one that you rode on earlier. Turn right and pedal back to the gate.

8.0 Reach the entrance gate.

8.3 Back to the parking lot.

South Cascades

This chapter, called South Cascades, could just as easily be entitled "Gifford Pinchot National Forest." Named in 1949 for the first chief of the USDA Forest Service, the Gifford Pinchot National Forest extends south from Mount Rainier to the Columbia River and was originally known as the Mount Rainier Forest Reserve when it was created in 1893.

The "G-P" includes several notable peaks—Mount St. Helens and Mount Adams among them—and some of the finest scenery in the state. Following the big bang that sheared 1,313 feet off the top of Mount St. Helens in 1980, the area surrounding it, including lands formerly owned by timber companies, became part of the Mount St. Helens Volcanic National Monument, which is administered by the USDA Forest Service.

A number of trails in the national monument are open to mountain bikes but are not included in this book. In order to travel into the monument area, visitors must pay an $8 entrance fee, good for three days.

For much of its length, the G-P straddles the east-west divide. This means it harbors a very diverse range of riding places, from the high alpine scenery typically found in eastern Washington to the wet, Douglas-fir and cedar forests of western Washington. The Forest Service does an admirable job of providing information for mountain bikers.

The forest is divided into two ranger districts—Cowlitz Valley (formerly Randle) and Mount Adams—and the national volcanic monument. There are also ranger stations at Packwood and Wind River. Much of the forest is actually closer to Portland than it is to Seattle. However, it is possible to undertake several of the rides in the Cowlitz Valley and Packwood Ranger Districts and get home to Pugetopolis by nightfall.

There are easily several dozen more rides waiting for you in the Gifford Pinchot National Forest, but the rides in this book are a representative sampling. Note also that as the Forest Service generally cuts back on road maintenance and building, many roads will be allowed to deteriorate. Some will likely be decommissioned. These situations may create more rides that are inaccessible to vehicles, but also create hazards beyond the scope of the average rider. Remember to check ahead before venturing out into mapped as well as uncharted territory.

Big Alpine Wanderlust

Location:	9 miles northeast of Trout Lake, in the Gifford Pinchot National Forest.
Distance:	17.9-mile loop.
Tread:	Gravel and packed dirt road, singletrack, some pavement.
Time:	4 to 5 hours.
Aerobic level:	Strenuous.
Technical difficulty:	3–4.
Best time to ride:	June to October.
Facilities:	None at trailhead.
Land status:	Gifford Pinchot National Forest, Mount Adams Ranger District.
Maps:	Gifford Pinchot National Forest, Mount Adams Ranger District.
Access:	From the Chevron station in Trout Lake, head north on Forest Road 17 for 1.3 miles until the fork with FR 23 (signed to Randle). Keep right. FR 17 branches right again in about a half-mile and then becomes FR 82. Follow it to the end of the pavement and turn right to the Sno-Park parking lot.

Notes on the Trail

It's no surprise that snowmobile riders and cross-country skiers saw the potential to make a series of loops from the logging roads in this area. When the snow is gone, the roads, including some of the marked winter trails, make for an ideal set of biking loops. The Big Alpine Loop includes a challenging section of singletrack that crosses the shoulder of McDonald Ridge. This ride provides a swatch of the fabric that makes up Washington alpine scenery—ponderosa pine, sage, and bell-clanging range cows! Note: This ride can also be ridden counter-clockwise.

The Ride

0.0 From the Sno-Park turn right on FR 82. Elevation 2,730 feet.
1.0 Road is nicely packed gravel shaded by tall conifers. Elevation 2,990 feet.

Big Alpine Wanderlust

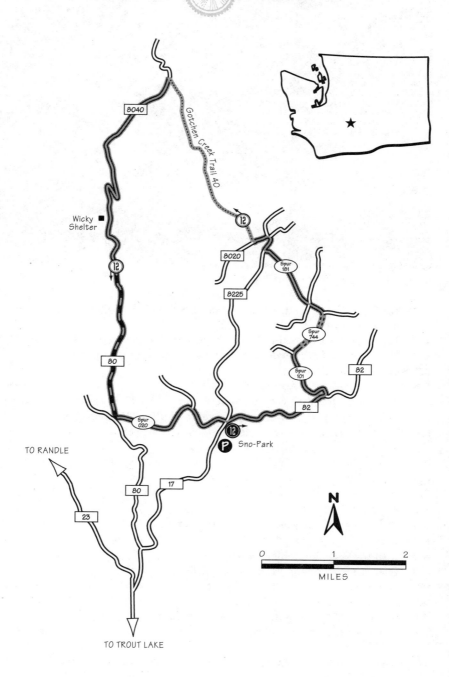

8040

Gotchen Creek Trail 40

12

Wicky Shelter

12

8020

Spur 181

8225

Spur 744

80

Spur 101

82

82

Spur 020

12

P Sno-Park

TO RANDLE

80

17

23

N

TO TROUT LAKE

0   1   2

MILES

Expect varied conditions on the Big Alpine ride.

1.7 Turn left on spur road 101. Sign states "Parking Lot 2." Elev. 3,180 feet. Surface changes to cinder.

2.7 Turn right on spur road 744. This is a jeep trail, rough in places but manageable. You'll soon ride through an open meadow frequented by range cattle.

3.4 Elevation 3,410 feet.

3.6 Junction. Go left onto spur road 181.

4.1 Wide area with four-way junction. Go straight across. Elevation 3,590 feet.

5.5 Go right at junction with main gravel road (FR 8225). Elevation 3,535 feet.

5.9 FR 8225 ends here. Proceed left and take a sharp left onto FR 8020. (If you see a sign indicating spur road 150 turn back.)

6.2 Turn right. The Gotchen Creek Trail 40 starts here. Elevation 3,590 feet.

6.8 Singletrack is loose and sandy. Elevation 3,715 feet.

7.0 Turnoff for Morrison Creek Trail. Keep on Trail 40.

7.2 Elevation 3,740 feet.

7.4 Cross a creek using the convenient log or ford it.

8.1 Cross a second creek. Elevation 3,880 feet.

8.2 Trail starts to climb. Elevation 3,940 feet.

8.8 Trail keeps climbing. Elevation 4,360 feet.

9.0 Trail peaks at 4,540 feet. There are a number of dying and dead standing trees there.

9.4 Reach FR 8040. Go left. Elevation 4,495 feet.

10.4 Gravel surface has some washboard areas. Ride at 12 m.p.h. or less. Elevation 4,175 feet.

11.8 Road gets rougher, but it's an effortless glide. Elevation 3,715 feet.

12.5 Pass the Wicky Shelter. Elevation 3,490 feet.

13.7 Elevation 3,150 feet.

14.3 Go straight onto the pavement. This is now FR 80.

15.9 Go left onto spur road 020. Sign indicates "Sno-Park 2 miles." Elevation 2,640 feet.

17.2 Keep right when 020 merges with spur road 041.

17.9 Return to parking lot.

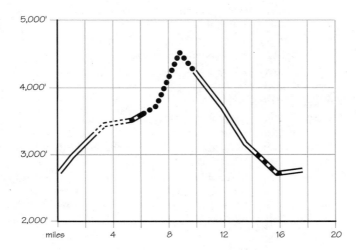

Middle Alpine Wanderlust

Location:	9 miles northeast of Trout Lake, in the Gifford Pinchot National Forest.
Distance:	10.7-mile loop.
Tread:	Gravel and dirt roads.
Time:	2 to 2.5 hours.
Aerobic level:	Moderate.
Technical difficulty:	2–3.
Best time to ride:	June to October.
Facilities:	None at trailhead.
Land status:	Gifford Pinchot National Forest, Mount Adams Ranger District.
Maps:	Gifford Pinchot National Forest, Mount Adams Ranger District
Access:	From the Chevron station in Trout Lake, head north on Forest Road 17 for 1.3 miles until the fork with FR 23 (signed to Randle). Keep right. FR 17 branches right again in about a half-mile and then becomes FR 82. Follow it to the end of the pavement and turn right to the Pineside Sno-Park. Park in the large lot set aside for winter recreation.

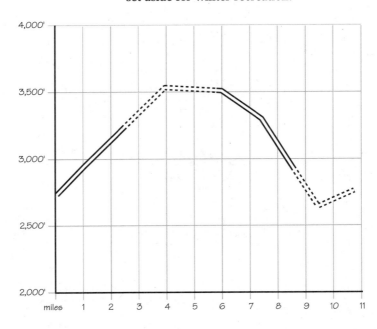

Middle Alpine Wanderlust

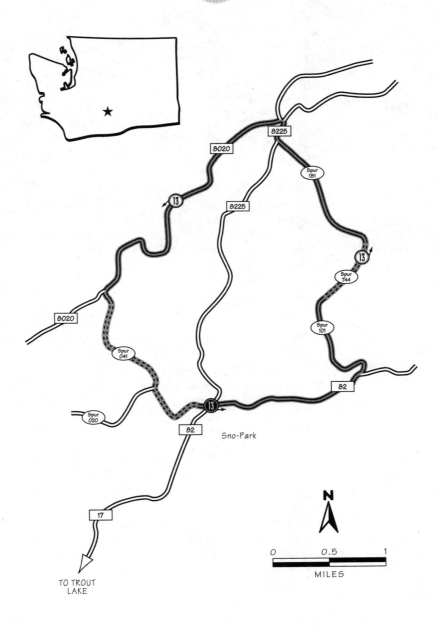

8225

8020

Spur
181

13

8225

13

Spur
744

8020

Spur
101

Spur
041

82

Sno-Park

Spur
020

82

17

N

0   0.5   1

MILES

TO TROUT
LAKE

An inquisitive herd grazes near the route of ride 13.

NOTES ON THE TRAIL

There are sufficient roads—mainly little-traveled—in this area that you can carve out numerous loops to suit your mood, the weather, the participants, or the phase of the moon. There's a loop for any reason and season. This ride fits in the middle, cutting out the hardest part of the Big Alpine ride but still providing lots of activity for your legs.

THE RIDE

0.0 From the Sno-Park turn right on FR 82. Elevation 2,730 feet.

1.0 Road is nicely packed gravel shaded by tall conifers. Elevation 2,990 feet.

1.7 Turn left on spur road 101. Sign states "Parking Lot 2." Elevation 3,180 feet. Surface changes to cinder.

2.7 Turn right on spur road 744. This is a jeep trail, rough in places but manageable. You'll soon ride through an open meadow frequented by range cattle.

3.4 Elevation 3,410 feet.

3.6 Junction. Go left onto spur road 181.

4.1 Wide area with four-way junction. Go straight across. Elevation 3,590 feet.

5.5 Go right at junction with main gravel road (FR 8225). Elevation 3,535 feet.

5.9 FR 8225 ends here. Proceed left and take a sharp left onto FR 8020. (If you see a sign indicating spur road 150 turn back.)

6.2 You'll pass the turn off for Trail 40 (Big Alpine ride). Elevation 3,575 feet. The descent begins.

7.5 Road surface turns from packed dirt to gravel. Elevation 3,280 feet.

8.4 Still rolling downhill. Elevation 2,980 feet.

8.8 Turn left on spur road 041. Elevation 2,870 feet.

9.9 Spur road 020 merges from the right. Keep on road 041. Elevation 2,685 feet.

10.7 Return to Sno-Park. Elevation 2,785 feet.

Little Alpine Wanderlust

Location:	9 miles northeast of Trout Lake, in the Gifford Pinchot National Forest.
Distance:	7.8-mile loop.
Tread:	Gravel and dirt roads.
Time:	1 to 1.5 hours.
Aerobic level:	Moderate.
Technical difficulty:	1.
Best time to ride:	June to October.
Facilities:	None.
Land status:	Gifford Pinchot National Forest, Mount Adams Ranger District.
Maps:	Gifford Pinchot National Forest, Mount Adams Ranger District.
Access:	From the Chevron station in Trout Lake, head north on Forest Road 17 for 1.3 miles until the fork with FR 23 (signed to Randle). Keep right. FR 17 branches right again in about a half-mile and then becomes FR 82. Follow it to the end of the pavement and turn right to the Pineside Sno-Park. Park in the large lot set aside for winter recreation.

NOTES ON THE TRAIL

When there are riders of mixed abilities in your group, you need a wider ride menu: one that offers a ride diet light on roots, rocks, and other obstacles that beginners may find overwhelming. This is the low-calorie ride that won't hobble a neophyte's enthusiasm for the sport. The climb involved helps ensure no one will be hungry for another ride immediately either.

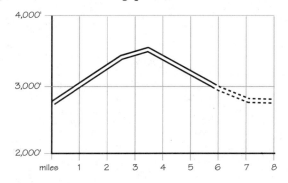

Little Alpine Wanderlust

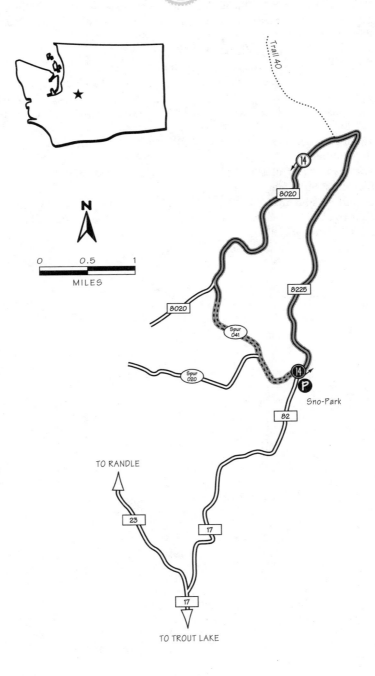

Trail 40

14

8020

8225

8020

Spur
041

Spur
020

14
P

Sno-Park

82

TO RANDLE

23

17

17

TO TROUT LAKE

N

0   0.5   1

MILES

THE RIDE

0.0 From the Sno-Park Trailhead, head straight up FR 8225. Elevation 2,780 feet.

0.5 There are some washboard ribs to contend with on the gravel road as you climb. Elevation 2,960 feet.

1.1 Alpine forest scenery. Elevation 3,095 feet.

1.4 Pass the end of spur road 101. Elevation 3,190 feet.

1.8 Mount Adams peeks its snowy head out as you get to 3,245 feet.

2.5 Elevation 3,400 feet.

3.2 Ride past the sign that says "End 8225" and then take an immediate left on FR 8020.

3.5 You'll pass the turnoff for Trail 40 (Big Alpine ride). Elevation 3,575 feet. The descent begins.

4.6 The road turns from dirt back to gravel. Elevation 3,280 feet.

5.5 Elevation 2,980 feet.

5.9 Go left on spur road 041. Elevation 2,870 feet.

7.0 Spur road 020 enters from the right. Keep straight. Elevation 2,685 feet.

7.8 Back to Sno-Park.

Buck Creek Loop

Location:	7 miles north of Trout Lake, in the Gifford Pinchot National Forest.
Distance:	13.8-mile loop.
Tread:	Singletrack, gravel and dirt roads, some pavement.
Time:	3.5 to 4 hours.
Aerobic level:	Moderate.
Technical difficulty:	2–3.
Best time to ride:	Trail is open from May 15 to November 1.
Facilities:	None.
Land status:	Gifford Pinchot National Forest, Mount Adams Ranger District.
Maps:	Gifford Pinchot National Forest, Mount Adams Ranger District.
Access:	From the Chevron station in Trout Lake, head north on Forest Road 17 for 3 miles. Keep right at the intersection with FR 23 and proceed uphill. Just over a mile later, turn left on FR 80. Follow it uphill until the first crossroads, where spur roads 031 and 020 meet. Turn right and park on 020.

NOTES ON THE TRAIL

Predictable rides are for those who love to roll along endless miles of black-top. Right? If you enjoy a surprise or two, Buck Creek is definitely the ride for you. It offers beautiful mature forest, a free-flowing river, technical areas, and a hill or two to keep you downshifting. The ride ends with a down-hill seemingly designed for mountain bikers.

THE RIDE

0.0 From your parking place on spur road 020, head across FR 80 onto spur road 031. Elevation 2,720 feet.

0.9 Reach Buck Creek trailhead. Elevation 2,840 feet.

1.2 Descend cautiously to a bridge across Wicky Creek. In summer, the tread is powdery soil. Elevation 2,735 feet. You're deep in the forest, about to climb up the sides of a narrow valley.

2.6 Elevation 2,885 feet.

Buck Creek Loop

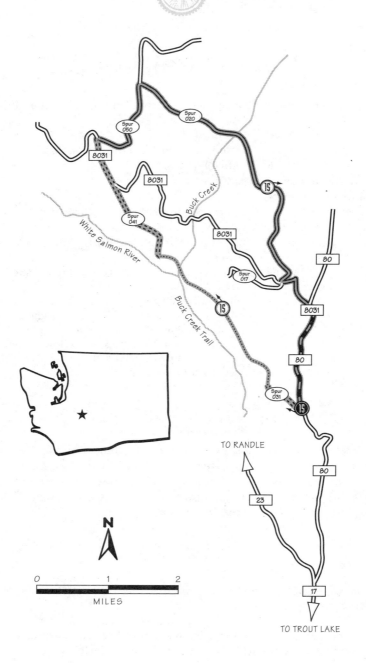

The trail up Buck Creek is less easy than it looks here.

2.8 White Salmon River becomes more visible as you begin to lose some of the height you just gained. Elevation 2,865 feet.

3.1 Cross creek. Elevation 2,840 feet.

3.3 Climb more steeply, still ridable for some. Elevation 3,000 feet.

3.5 Trailhead. Turn right on spur road 041. This particular 041 is a doubletrack gravel road with grass growing in the middle. Elevation 3,140 feet.

4.0 Surface changes to loose gravel, then crushed gravel and cinder as you ascend a small hill. Elevation 3,330 feet.

4.4 Thanks to recent logging, you get a great view of Mount Adams. Elevation 3,405 feet.

4.6 Junction with FR 8031. Go left. Elevation 3,415 feet.

5.5 You'll see a sign "Crofton Butte Trail 73." Turn right onto spur road 050 and proceed uphill. Elevation 3,400 feet.

7.0 Turn right on spur road 020. (Notice how it has the worn tread. It's the only road out from this point.) Elevation 3,725 feet.

8.0 After passing a plantation and cut area, re-enter the woods. Elevation 3,820 feet.

9.0 As you gain elevation you'll see that you're riding in a huge natural bowl formed by several valleys. Looking south you can see Mount Hood sticking its snowy snout into the air. Elevation 3,865 feet.

10.0 Packed gravel makes for a smooth descent. But watch out for loose sections. Elevation 3,560 feet.

11.0 Elevation 3,345 feet.

11.5 Four-way junction. Go left on FR 8031.

12.2 Junction. Turn right (downhill) on paved FR 80.

13.8 Glide blissfully back to your car on the hardtop.

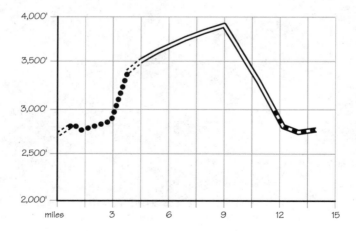

Council Lake

Location:	52 miles east of Cougar; 33 miles south of Randle; 23 miles north of Trout Lake, in the Gifford Pinchot National Forest.
Distance:	7.7-mile loop.
Tread:	Singletrack, dirt and gravel forest roads.
Time:	2 to 3 hours.
Aerobic level:	Moderate to strenuous.
Technical difficulty:	3.
Best time to ride:	June to October.
Facilities:	Vault toilets at Council Lake Campground.
Land status:	Gifford Pinchot National Forest, Mount Adams Ranger District.
Maps:	Gifford Pinchot National Forest, Mount Adams Ranger District.
Access:	From Seattle, drive Interstate 5 south to Woodland. Go east on Washington Route 503 to Cougar, where the road (still paved) becomes Forest Road 90. Keep heading east until the junction with FR 23. Turn north (left) toward Randle. Drive FR 23 for just over 3 miles to FR 2334. Turn left. In less than a mile, take a right on spur road 016, signed to Council Lake Campground. The campground can be busy on summer weekends. If there's no space, park at the junction of roads 016 and 2334.

NOTES ON THE TRAIL

Sometimes a ride doesn't have to be long to be memorable. What you will recall most about this ride is the eyeful of Mount Adams you get. It's a stunning mountain resplendent in a white jacket that, in the right conditions, glistens with the afternoon sun. The mountain is actually out of sight when you start up a jeep road from the campground, but 2 miles later, boom, it's there. If you don't marvel at this snowy mass, consider an alternative activity (maybe indoors). Just so that you don't ogle too much at the mountain, there are tricky corners, trail hazards, and some interesting downhill to negotiate. In late summer, expect the trail surface to be like talcum.

Council Lake

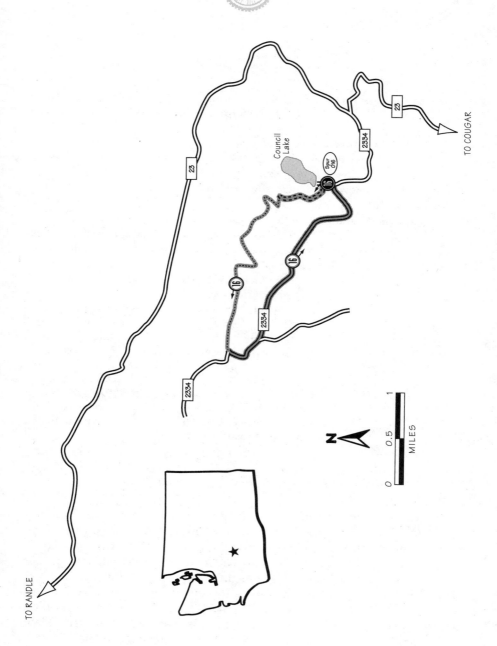

THE RIDE

0.0 From the campground, proceed uphill to the west away from the lake. Elevation 4,215 feet.

0.5 The jeep road climbs steeply and is rough in places. Elevation 4,475 feet.

1.0 Elevation 4,695 feet.

1.3 You reach a small clearing. A hiking trail leads off to the top of the mountain. Keep straight, entering the start of the singletrack.

2.0 Watch for big rocks on the trail and other obstacles. There's a drop-off on one side that demands care and attention.

2.3 There sits the mountain. Stop if you want to admire the view.

2.8 Smooth trail descends into thicker forest. Elevation 4,265 feet.

3.2 Lots of bumps as you slowly lose altitude. Elevation 4,125 feet.

3.5 Elevation 4,000 feet as you traverse alpine scenery.

3.7 The valley bottoms at 3,915 feet as you enter a forest of young trees offering limited shade.

4.5 Reach FR 2334. Turn left. Elevation 4,195 feet.

5.1 Junction with FR 9091. Keep left on FR 2334, and start to climb.

6.0 Climb peaks and you begin the cruise down to the campground road.

7.4 Turn left on spur road 016 for the campground. Elevation 4,185 feet.

7.7 Return to campground.

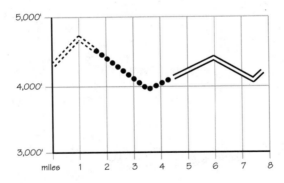

Krause Ridge Loop

Location:	6.6 miles southwest of Randle, in the Gifford Pinchot National Forest.
Distance:	13.5-mile loop.
Tread:	Singletrack, dirt and gravel roads.
Time:	2.5 to 3 hours.
Aerobic level:	Moderate.
Technical difficulty:	2–3.
Best time to ride:	May to October.
Facilities:	None.
Land status:	Gifford Pinchot National Forest, Cowlitz Valley Ranger District.
Maps:	Gifford Pinchot National Forest, Cowlitz Valley Ranger District (formerly Randle Ranger District).
Access:	From Seattle, drive south on Interstate 5 for 18 miles to Washington Route 516. Follow it east to the West Valley Highway (WA 167). Proceed south through Puyallup, continuing on WA 161 through Eatonville to the junction with WA 7. Head east to Elbe and then south until WA 7 meets U.S. Highway 12 at Morton. Turn left and go east 17 miles to Randle. Turn right (south) on WA 131 and about a mile later, take the left fork on FR 23. In 5.6 miles, turn right on FR 2306. Follow it for a mile and park at the trailhead sign.

NOTES ON THE TRAIL

When the sun shines in late spring many trails are still out-of-bounds because of snow. Not to worry. The Krause Ridge trail is a low-elevation ride that has lots of appeal: old-growth forest, views, and some sweet singletrack. Expect some mud if you go early in the season. Expect to have a good time no matter what time of year you ride it, making allowances for snow, of course. This ride describes a loop of nearby roads; it's also possible to shorten the ride by choosing other roads or by simply completing the singletrack portion as an out-and-back.

Krause Ridge Loop

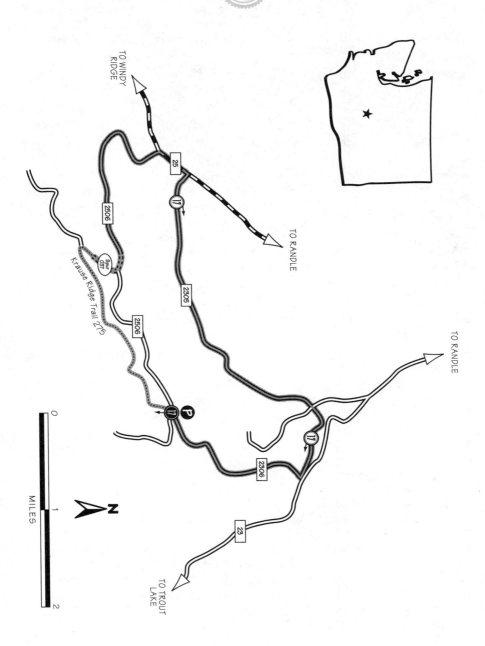

TO WINDY RIDGE

25

17

TO RANDLE

2506

Spur 037

2505

Krause Ridge Trail 275

2506

TO RANDLE

17

17

2506

23

TO TROUT LAKE

MILES

0   1   2

N

Ah, smell the loamy singletrack on an early morning ride to Krause Ridge.

THE RIDE

0.0 Krause Ridge Trailhead (Trail 275). Elevation 1,360.

1.0 The forest can be dark at the start. The trail climbs gently through old-growth. Elevation 1,720 feet.

1.3 Stiffer section of climbing. Elevation 2,000.

1.4 Cross FR 2506 and proceed uphill on the singletrack.

1.5 Start to descend through a fern-enclosed trail that's narrow and intimate.

2.2 Elevation 2,015 feet.

2.6 Watch for a small spur trail on the left that leads to a point affording a bird's eye view over the Cispus River. Tower Rock stands proudly above the surrounding trees.

2.8 Begin another descent, which features a series of hairpin bends.

3.2 Trail keeps rolling downhill with enough elevation loss to propel you but not enough to make you grab at the brakes continuously.

3.5 Elevation 1,660 feet.

3.8 Enter a clear-cut area, where the understory of vegetation is thriving on the extra light and moisture. Elevation 1,625 feet.

4.7 Emerge onto spur road 037. Go right.

5.2 Junction with FR 2506. Go left, and enjoy an exhilarating downhill. (For a shorter loop, you could turn right here.)

7.6 Junction with FR 25 (paved). Turn right.

8.0 Take first right on FR 2305.

8.9 This is a good road of packed gravel that parallels Ames Creek.

11.5 Junction. Keep straight. Some uphill ahead. Elevation 1,000 feet.

12.2 Elevation 1,260 feet.

12.4 As you come up the final stretch of hill you'll see paved FR 23. Keep right on the dirt road and turn right for FR 2306.

13.5 Road to trailhead climbs slightly through a mixed area of open new forest and older trees. Reach your vehicle at the trailhead.

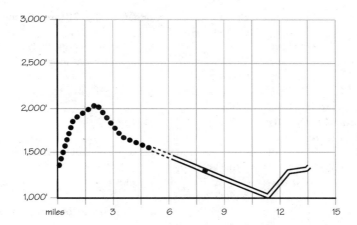

Lewis River

Location:	25 miles east of Cougar, in the Gifford Pinchot National Forest.
Distance:	11.9 miles, one way; 22.6-mile loop via paved road.
Tread:	Singletrack for the one-way ride; loop includes some paved road.
Time:	3 hours one-way; 4.5 hours round-trip.
Aerobic level:	Moderate.
Technical difficulty:	2–3.
Best time to ride:	June to October.
Facilities:	Primitive toilets and water at Lower Falls Campground.
Land status:	Gifford Pinchot National Forest, Mount Adams Ranger District.
Maps:	Gifford Pinchot National Forest, Mount Adams Ranger District.
Access:	From Seattle, drive south on Interstate 5 to Woodland. Go east on Washington Route 503 to Cougar, where the road (still paved) becomes Forest Road 90. Drive east for approximately 25 miles to the Lower Falls Campground. Display an annual parking pass or pay the day fee to park there.

Notes on the trail

All the drama of the Northwest is represented here: old-growth western redcedar, bigleaf maples, ferns, dry creeks, a mineral-rich river, and, naturally, hills that go up and down. To keep the plot interesting, there are also twists and turns, as well as unexpected obstacles. In short, you are in for a good experience, challenging in parts but with high ratings on the enjoyment quotient as you zip up one incline, cruise down another and then negotiate a tricky turn. It's what mountain bikes are made for. I should mention that I saw a black bear some distance off the trail.

Lewis River

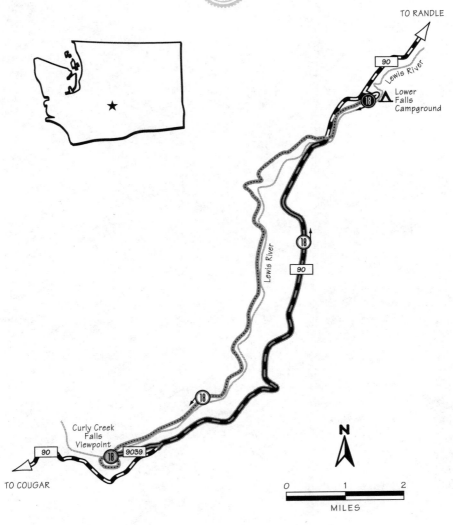

TO RANDLE

90

Lewis River

18

Lower
Falls
Campground

18

90

Lewis River

18

Curly Creek
Falls
Viewpoint

90   18   9039

TO COUGAR

N

0   1   2

MILES

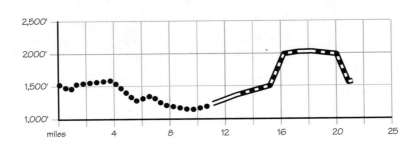

2,500'

2000'

1,500'

1,000'

miles   4   8   12   16   20   25

Singletrack hardly comes better than on the meandering trail of the Lewis River.

0.0 Proceed to the entrance of Lower Falls Campground and pick up the trail on the left. Elevation 1,530 feet.

0.1 Keep right at the fork and follow the river downstream through an understory of ferns.

1.0 Elevation 1,420 feet.

1.3 Unmarked trail, keep right.

1.4 Cross FR 90. Trail continues slightly to your right.

1.5 Elevation 1,520 feet.

1.8 Descend to creek crossing. Watch for tight corner. Elevation 1,410 feet.

2.4 After another uphill, drop back to 1,420 feet. Take a moment to enjoy the calm beauty of the forest.

3.2 Cross a bridge with broken slats. Elevation 1,560 feet.

3.5 River overlook. Definitely stop now. Elevation 1,600 feet.

3.7 Another bridge. Elevation 1,680 feet.

3.8 Log bridge. Keep right to ford narrow stream or walk across log. Get ready for a rapid descent that brings you back in sight of the river.

4.3 It's wet alongside the river even in mid-summer. Elevation 1,380 feet.

5.3 Expect to see the remains of a downed Douglas-fir. Elevation 1,345 feet.

6.1 The trail is now rolling more gently.

6.6 Cross a bridge at elevation 1,280 feet and prepare for a quick climb to 1,305 feet.

7.1 Elevation 1,325 feet.

7.6 Remnants of huge cedars destroyed in a landslide.

8.1 The forest opens up to reveal lots of light. Elevation 1,215 feet.

8.8 Bolt Camp Shelter, rustic backpacker accommodations by the river.

10.0 Roll through a forest of younger trees.

10.7 Start a short climb. Elevation 1,190 feet.

11.5 Emerge onto FR 9039. Cross the road to continuation of trail.

11.9 Reach viewpoint at Curly Creek Falls. You can marvel at the two natural bridges eroded into the rocks on the opposite bank of the Lewis River. You may choose to end the ride here or complete a loop by riding back on FR 90, which is a quiet, paved road. To continue the loop, turn right onto FR 9039 and head back down the hill and across the river.

12.9 Junction with FR 90. Go left on the paved road. Elevation 1,370 feet.

14.2 Elevation 1,410 feet.

15.9 Elevation 1,865 feet.

17.0 Cross Big Creek. Elevation 2,005 feet.

20.5 Start of short gravel section. Elevation 2,005 feet. After the road turns back into pavement, it swoops downhill.

21.3 Cross Lewis River. Elevation 1,500 feet.

22.6 Turn right into campground.

East Canyon Ridge Loop

Location:	About 30 miles southeast of Randle, in the Gifford Pinchot National Forest.
Distance:	12.2-mile loop.
Tread:	Gravel logging road, dirt singletrack, some pavement.
Time:	2.5 to 3.5 hours.
Aerobic level:	Moderate.
Technical difficulty:	3. Skilled.
Best time to ride:	Late May to October.
Facilities:	None.
Land status:	Gifford Pinchot National Forest, Cowlitz Valley Ranger District.
Maps:	Gifford Pinchot National Forest, Cowlitz Valley Ranger District.
Access:	From Seattle, drive south on Interstate 5 for 18 miles to Washington Route 516. Follow it east to the West Valley Highway (WA 167). Proceed south through Puyallup, continuing on WA 161 through Eatonville until the junction with WA 7. Head east to Elbe and then south until WA 7 meets U.S. Highway 12 at Morton. Turn left and go east 17 miles to Randle. Turn right (south) on WA 131 and about a mile later, take the left fork on Forest Road 23. Continue on FR 23 for approximately 30 miles until you reach the junction with FR 2328. Park on FR 2328. If you come to the sign pointing to the Chain of Lakes area on FR 2329 you've gone about a mile too far on FR 23.

NOTES ON THE TRAIL

One of the great pleasures about riding in the Gifford Pinchot National Forest is you often have its trails to yourself. For your own private Washington with a good mix of riding conditions, pick East Canyon Ridge. It offers a respectable climb, some tough downhill sections, a sprinkling of mud, and views from the ridge to gulp in along with fine mountain air. And let's not forget the kind of singletrack you wish was just around the corner instead of a three-hour drive away. (But then if it was, you'd have to share it with others.) Note that motorcycles use this trail.

East Canyon Ridge Loop

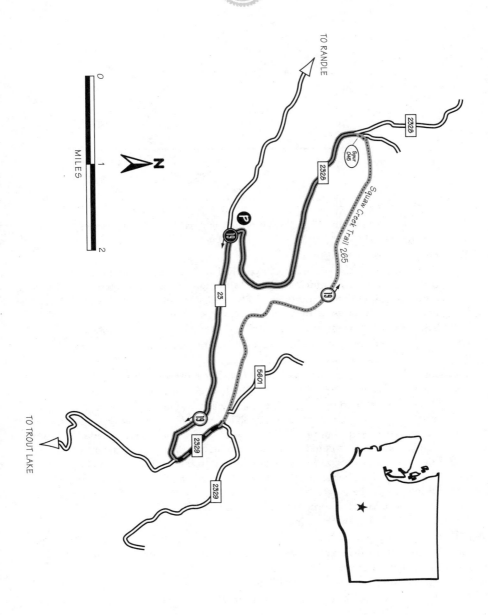

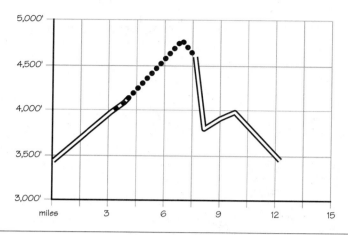

THE RIDE

0.0 Ride up the mainline road FR 23, which is gravel here. Elevation 3,425 feet.

3.0 Left on paved FR 2329.

3.8 Keep left on FR 5601.

4.0 Turn left onto Trail 265, East Canyon Ridge. You'll be gladdened to see a sign banning all-terrain vehicles (ATVs), although occasionally you may still see motorcycles, which are permitted. The trail starts off soft and sandy but won't present any traction difficulties. Elevation 4,155 feet.

4.4 Begin a brief descent, gentle at first and then over exposed roots.

4.9 Steep descent dumps you 55 feet lower in the same distance, or so it seems.

5.1 Wooden walkway over wetlands.

5.2 Start climbing again. See evidence of earlier motorcycle use.

5.8 The first top. Elevation 4,515 feet. The last section is very steep and difficult. You may be able to ride but you'll likely walk. Either way, the ball-bearing-size pumice underfoot makes it tricky. Nice sample of sub-alpine species here enjoying the brief summers with a flurry of colors. Great views of Mount Rainier and the carpeted forest of the Gifford Pinchot. Be aware of the cliff edge. The next section has you side-hilling to the peak.

6.4 The "real" top. Elevation 4,780 feet. You cross a steep slope of exposed rock which prudence suggests to walk. It's best you agree with prudence. After some more viewing, prepare for the descent.

6.6 Rock-faced turn cambers inconsiderately the wrong way.

7.0 Just another panorama.

7.7 The hill drops off sharply here. Keep your tires and your eyes on the trail.

7.8 You begin to move off the rocky ridge and back among the forested soils, churned in places by motorcyclists.

8.1 Steep section with loose soil that ultimately brings you out on a spur road. Elevation 3,800 feet.

8.4 Look for sign that says "Trail Follows Road for 1.5 miles." The sign only applies if you are continuing on Trail 265, but you're not. Turn left and ride the spur road until the intersection. Then go left on FR 2328, which starts gently uphill and back in the direction from whence you came.

9.0 You'll appreciate the smooth-packed dirt surface of the road after the jostling descent on the trail. Elevation 3,870 feet.

9.7 If the clouds cooperate, Rainier looms large. Elevation (your's, not the mountain's) 3,975 feet.

10.0 Start the descent back to your car. The road on the downhill becomes a little rougher but not enough to ruin the fun.

12.2 Back to the parking spot.

Surprise Lake Loop

Location:	10 miles west of Trout Lake, in the Gifford Pinchot National Forest.
Distance:	9-mile loop.
Tread:	Dirt and gravel road, singletrack.
Time:	2 to 2.5 hours.
Aerobic level:	Moderate.
Technical difficulty:	2–4.
Best time to ride:	Trail is open June 1 to November 15.
Facilities:	None.
Land status:	Gifford Pinchot National Forest, Mount Adams Ranger District.
Maps:	Gifford Pinchot National Forest, Mount Adams Ranger District.
Access:	Drive north through Trout Lake on Washington Route 141. After 1.6 miles, turn right on Forest Road 88. Drive 5.8 miles farther and turn left on FR 8821. (Watch for a Sno-Park area on the right.) Drive uphill and stay on FR 8821 for 3.5 miles until you reach the marked trailhead.

NOTES ON THE TRAIL

Picture for a moment what this area must have looked like when the only visitors were Indians who came each year to harvest the bountiful huckleberries that thrive at this altitude. Of course, the roads that snake through this high plateau allow you easier access, as well as the throngs of berry-pickers, hunters, and motorists looking for some forest drives. But if you pick your ride time carefully you can avoid most of the crowds. And the ride is well worth it. It's described here as a loop, which means half is on the aforementioned gravel roads. Unless you're into truly punishing rides, you'll want to ride the singletrack in the direction laid out here. One other note about this ride: The surprise is that you may not actually see a lake.

Surprise Lake Loop

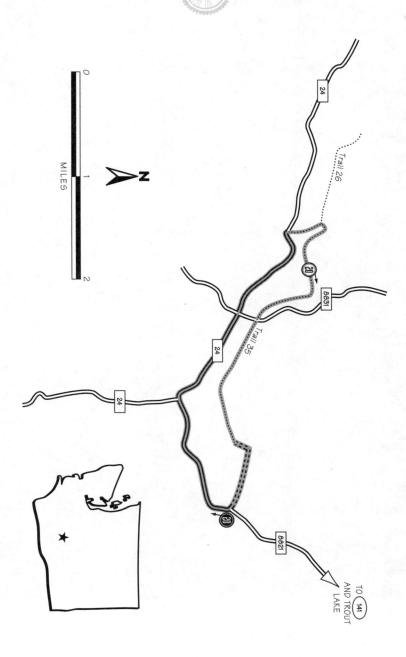

On the way back to Surprise Lake trailhead.

THE RIDE

0.0 Park at the trailhead and head uphill on FR 8821. Elevation 2,820 feet.

0.6 The gravel road is in reasonable shape. Elevation 2,900 feet.

1.4 Junction. Turn right on FR 24. Elevation 2,830 feet.

2.5 Four-way junction. Keep straight, following signs for "Sawtooth Berry Fields."

3.4 Elevation 2,895 feet.

3.9 Road begins to climb more. Elevation 3,015 feet.

4.3 Turn right on Trail 26. You'll see a trailhead sign. Elevation 3,130 feet.

4.6 Cross stream and just beyond it you'll see the junction with Trail 35. Turn right. Elevation 3,140 feet.

4.7 Trail 35 is sandy in places and soft. It descends and crosses a creek bed.

5.0 Evidence of motorcycle damage. Elevation 3,080 feet.

6.0 There's enough elevation drop to propel you along virtually without pedaling. Paying attention is crucial, however. Elevation 2,860 feet.

6.2 Creek crossing. Hard to ride through. Trail climbs up on the other side.

6.5 Keep left on main trail.

6.8 Cross FR 8831. Elevation 2,775 feet.

7.8 The trail widens to become a jeep road, then enters a meadow. Re-emerges as a narrow trail through a forest of grand old trees. Elevation 2,780 feet.

8.3 Trail shows signs of over-use by motorcycles and four-wheelers here. Elevation 2,730 feet.

9.0 Reach the trailhead.

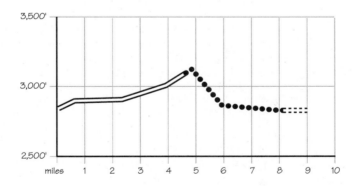

Tongue Mountain Loop

Location:	About 10 miles south of Randle, in the Gifford Pinchot National Forest.
Distance:	17-mile loop.
Tread:	Packed gravel and dirt logging roads, forest singletrack, some pavement.
Time:	4.5 to 5.5 hours.
Aerobic level:	Strenuous.
Technical difficulty:	2–4.
Best time to ride:	May to October.
Facilities:	None, but camping nearby (no water).
Land status:	Gifford Pinchot National Forest, Cowlitz Valley Ranger District.
Maps:	Gifford Pinchot National Forest, Cowlitz Valley Ranger District (formerly Randle Ranger District).
Access:	From Seattle, drive south on Interstate 5 to the intersection with Washington Route 12. Go east toward Yakima, passing through Morton. Upon entering Randle, turn right (south) on WA 131 toward Mount St. Helens. Just beyond the Cowlitz River bridge, bear left on Forest Road 23. In 9.3 miles, turn right on FR 28. Pass the Yellowjacket Pond picnic area on the right and then turn left on FR 29. Park in the wide space at the intersection or back at the picnic area.

NOTES ON THE TRAIL

This ride's like those chewy chocolate-filled candies: tough on the outside with a satisfying taste on the inside that lingers long after you've swallowed. The hard part on this ride is the long cartilage-grinding haul up to the logging road to the start of the trail. The moist chocolate part is the delicious descent through an ancient forest that survived a huge forest fire in the 1920s. The downhill is steep in places, and since the trail is also open to motorcyclists, the loamy forest soil can get churned up, making descents very interesting. A great workout ride with some wonderful forest trail and plunging descents. Think Belgian chocolate.

Tongue Mountain Loop

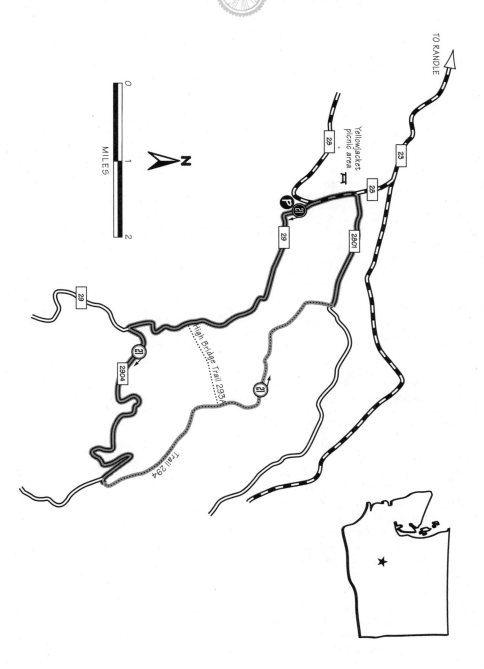

TO RANDLE

Yellowjacket
picnic area

28

23

28

29

2801

P

21

29

21

2904

High Bridge Trail 293

Trail 294

21

MILES

N

0   1   2

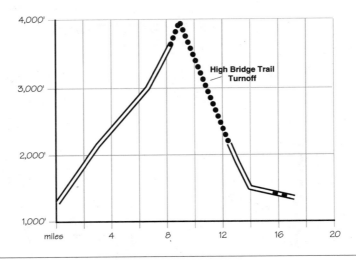

4,000'

3,000'

High Bridge Trail
Turnoff

2,000'

1,000'

miles   4   8   12   16   20

THE RIDE

0.0 Proceed up the cartilage-grinding FR 29. Elevation 1,250 feet.

2.9 Pass the trailhead for the High Bridge Trail (293A). Elevation 2,150 feet.

3.8 Left on FR 2904.

5.0 Elevation 2,660 feet.

6.9 As you reach 3,000 feet, look to the left to see an elaborate dam-building feat by beavers.

8.0 Go left on trail 294. Sign the trail register, and shift into the lowest gear. Elevation 3,735 feet.

8.7 Elevation 4,000 feet.

9.0 Junction for hikers-only trail to the summit. If you want to take a look, stash your bike and walk.

9.2 Steep downhill section with soft tread.

9.8 Get a brief glimpse of what you've toiled up from this vista spot on the trail. Elevation 3,585 feet.

10.1 Exhilarating luge-like downhill that requires care and skill to descend safely, and an eye for ascending motorcyclists.

10.2 Junction with High Bridge Trail (293A). For a 1.5-mile return to the other end of this trail on road 29, take a left here. (See ride notes on following page.) Otherwise, keep on the straight and narrow.

10.5 Enter an area of widely spaced old forest with a verdant carpet of undergrowth. Look for the burned relics from the great forest fires of 1902 and 1918.

10.7 The trail drops steeply, losing about one foot of vertical for practically every foot you travel.

11.4 Cross from the north of the ridge and begin a series of switchbacks as you make your way back down to the lower valley. Prepare to drop a couple of hundred feet in the next 0.2 mile.

12.0 There's an incredibly sharp turn here as you descend. If the soil is loose, consider walking.

12.9 Elevation 1,890 feet. Stop if you want to marvel at the verdant richness of the forest understory here.

13.8 Pop out on road 2801 and turn left. Elevation 1,425 feet.

15.4 Junction of 2801 and FR 28. Go left.

17.0 Go left on FR 29 and return to your vehicle.

HIGH BRIDGE TRAIL OPTION

For a shorter ride involving less climbing, but less thrilling singletrack, drive to the High Bridge Trail on road 29. Follow the directions above, taking the left turn at 10.2 miles. The High Bridge Trail drops steeply then levels out through an attractive wetland area before returning you to road 29. Mileage this way is 8.9, which you can cover in 2.5 to 3 hours.

Trout Creek Hill

Location:	About 10 miles northeast of Carson, in the Gifford Pinchot National Forest.
Distance:	10.3-mile loop.
Tread:	Gravel road.
Time:	2.5 to 3 hours.
Aerobic level:	Moderate.
Technical difficulty:	1–2.
Best time to ride:	May to October.
Facilities:	None.
Land status:	Gifford Pinchot National Forest, Wind River Ranger District.
Maps:	Gifford Pinchot National Forest, Wind River Ranger District.
Access:	From Interstate 205 in Vancouver, head east on Washington Route 14 for 46 miles to the exit for Carson. Head north through town on Forest Road 54. After 8 miles, turn left on Hemlock Road and follow signs to the Wind River Ranger Station. Just beyond the ranger station, turn right on FR 43 (which turns from paved to gravel) and proceed until you see FR 4303 on the right. Park near the intersection, taking care not to block the gate.

NOTES ON THE TRAIL

Trout Creek Hill is a small outcropping detached from the surrounding hills. This area is set aside by the Forest Service for research and forest experimentation, which is why the gate at the bottom of FR 4303 is usually closed to motor traffic. This makes for a quiet ride on a loop that could have been devised by someone with a penchant for Victorian mazes. This ride pretty much allows you to circumnavigate the hill and conquer it, too. An easy ride for most cyclists, it does have a couple of steeper sections and areas where the gravel requires bike-handling skills.

Trout Creek Hill

TO 12

MILES

0

0.5

1

N

4306

22

Spur
413

Spur
414

22

4303

4303

P

22

43

TO CARSON

Trees block any view of the surrounding forest from the top of Trout Creek Hill.

0.0 Proceed around the gate and up FR 4303, which is a good gravel and dirt road.

0.3 Junction. Keep right. Elevation 1,135 feet.

0.9 Junction. Go left on spur road 413. Elevation 1,270 feet.

3.1 The road continues to climb gradually as it rounds the hill. As you get higher, the views get better.

3.6 Still rounding and climbing but with a brief descent ahead. Elevation 1,535 feet.

3.7 Large area with four-way junction. Keep straight. You now rejoin FR 4303. Elevation 1,490 feet.

5.1 Junction. Go right (uphill) on spur road 414. This is the final climb to the summit.

5.8 Views over the surrounding valleys emerge as you gain height. Sections of loose, large rocks here. Elevation 1,669 feet.

6.9 Emerge into an open, wooded flat area of mature trees. This is the top. You can explore the top for awhile, but you must eventually turn around for the ride back. Elevation 2,115 feet.

8.8 Junction. Turn right (on FR 4303). You're now heading downhill on the east side of the hill. Elevation 1,900 feet.

9.4 Spur road 413 merges from the right. Keep heading downhill on the good surface. Elevation 1,310 feet.

10.3 Return to gate and parked vehicle.

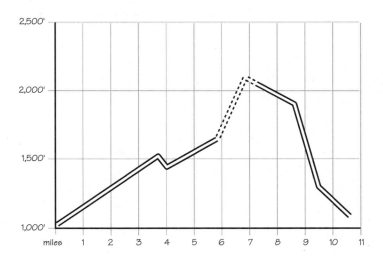

North Cascades

Mount Baker is the snowy summit that beckons to travelers heading north on Interstate 5. Farther south, Mount Pilchuck sticks its craggy shoulder above the surrounding farmlands. To the east is the ridge of the Cascades.

Between the flatlands bordering the interstate and the peaks of the Cascades there is some fine riding. Large tracts of the forest here are under private ownership; public access is permitted but normally restricted to weekends. Luckily, the Mount Baker-Snoqualmie and Wenatchee National Forests also have extensive holdings.

First, a confession: This chapter is slimmer than it should rightfully be. There were a good dozen rides among the portfolio in contention when I began planning this chapter. Alas, time and weather caught up with my research. Several rides that I had taken previously had to be omitted since I was unable to revisit and confirm them in time for publication.

The four rides that did make it in represent all the categories in this book —from the easy interurban rail-trail, to the challenging singletrack of Blanchard, to the logging roads of Derby and Walker Canyons. There are plenty more rides close to Darrington, Skykomish, and Sedro-Woolley.

Many rides on the western flank of the Cascades are within a two-hour drive of the Puget Sound urban area via I-5. Heading farther east will require proportionately more driving time as both Washington 20 (North Cascades Highway) and U.S. Highway 2 are two-lane roads for most of their length across the mountains. Make allowances for this when you are planning your rides.

Blanchard Hill Loop

Location:	14 miles northeast of Mount Vernon.
Distance:	8.4-mile loop.
Tread:	Gravel logging road, dirt singletrack.
Time:	2.5 to 3.5 hours.
Aerobic level:	Strenuous.
Technical difficulty:	5.
Best time to ride:	June to October.
Facilities:	None at trailhead.
Land status:	DNR.
Maps:	USGS Alger.
Access:	From Seattle, drive north on Interstate 5 beyond Mount Vernon. Just south of Bellingham, take the exit signed for Alger. Turn left and drive 0.4 mile to Barrel Springs Road. Go left and drive for 0.7 mile until you see a sign on the right for Blanchard Mountain. Turn onto the gravel road and park at the first trailhead.

NOTES ON THE TRAIL

Blanchard is an orphan hill that towers over the Skagit Valley delta. The land is owned by the Washington Department of Natural Resources, which has logged areas on this and neighboring hills. Consequently, the approach does not look very inviting—a wide gravel road and scrub vegetation. The upper reaches of Blanchard witnessed the saws long enough ago that it may be a few years yet before the area is again ripe for logging. Take this ride while you can. The going is tough in places; the views are outstanding; and the uphill tread is nicely compacted forest floor. In contrast, the downhill is rough and filled with hazards. But then that makes it all part of the adventure. Note: Part of the descent includes an unmaintained trail.

THE RIDE

0.0 From the parking lot (the first you come to on the entrance road), continue up the main road. Elevation 440 feet.

1.2 The road forks here. Keep right.

1.3 Turn left onto trail. Elevation 625 feet.

Blanchard Hill

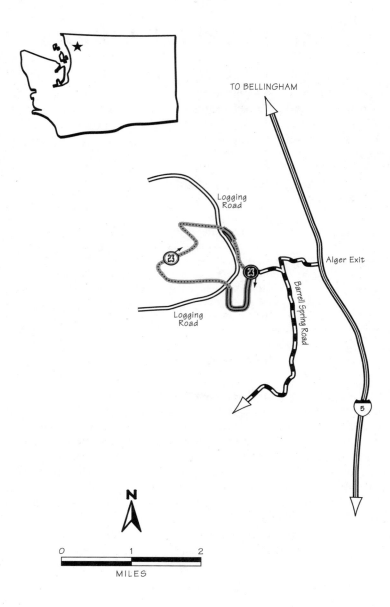

TO BELLINGHAM

Logging Road

Alger Exit

Barrell Spring Road

Logging Road

N

0   1   2
MILES

Blanchard Hill sits high above the surrounding farmland of the Skagit Valley.

1.6 Cross a wooden bridge.

2.3 First of what will be a series of switchbacks. Elevation 955 feet.

2.7 Junction with PNW Trail to Samish Overlook. Stay on original trail. Elevation 1,155 feet.

3.2 Trail is rock-strewn. Elevation 1,380 feet.

3.5 Cross bridge and then descend slightly before next bridge. Elevation 1,560 feet.

4.2 Junction. Turn right for Lizard Lake. Trail follows course of an old logging railroad, complete with bumps created by the railroad ties. Elevation 1,770 feet.

4.8 Junction. Turn left for Lizard Lake.

4.9 Park your bike and walk the few yards down to the lakeshore. There is a horse camp here, and don't be surprised to see equestrians. Turnaround and head back to the junction where you just turned. Elevation 1,640 feet.

5.1 Junction. Turn left and proceed downhill. Elevation 1,650 feet.

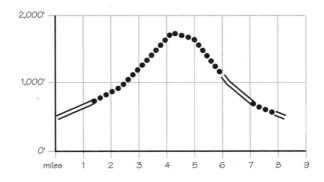

5.3 Unmarked junction. Look to your left for a sign that says "Alternative Incline B1000" and follow that route to the left. This trail is not maintained by the DNR.

5.6 The route of all roots. This section is criss-crossed with tree roots. Elevation 1,490 feet.

6.2 Beginning of a steep section with loose soil and rocks. Elevation 1,065 feet.

6.3 Reach the sanctuary of a gravel road. Turn right (downhill). Elevation 940 feet.

7.4 After breezing down the gravel (compared to wheezing down the root-infested trail), slow down after a mile and look for a broad area sometimes used for parking. Turn left here and you'll see a trail lead off into the scrub-woods. This is a roller-coaster singletrack that drops you through a logging area now overgrown with fireweeds and alder. Elevation 675 feet.

8.1 Reach main gravel road. Turn left. Elevation 430 feet.

8.4 Back to your vehicle.

Derby Canyon Loop

Location:	About 7 miles east of Leavenworth, in the Wenatchee National Forest.
Distance:	18.8-mile loop.
Tread:	Packed dirt and gravel roads.
Time:	4.5 to 5.5 hours.
Aerobic level:	Moderate to strenuous.
Technical difficulty:	2.
Best time to ride:	May to October.
Facilities:	None.
Land status:	Wenatchee National Forest, Leavenworth Ranger District.
Maps:	Green Trails Leavenworth (incomplete); Leavenworth Ranger District map.
Access:	From Leavenworth, drive 6 miles east on U.S. Highway 2 until Peshastin. Turn left at the light and cross the river. Proceed along the main street under the railway bridge. Turn right and parallel the tracks for 1.5 miles. Where the road turns left is the start of Derby Canyon. Follow the road north until it turns from pavement to dirt. About a half-mile later Forest Road 7400 begins. The first part of the road serves local residents. Don't park in the open area near the fenced pasture. Instead, drive a little farther until there is a safe pull-off within the forest boundary.

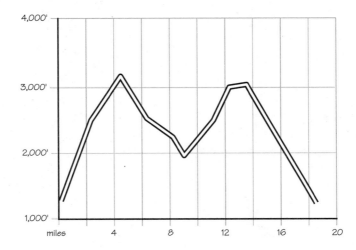

Derby Canyon

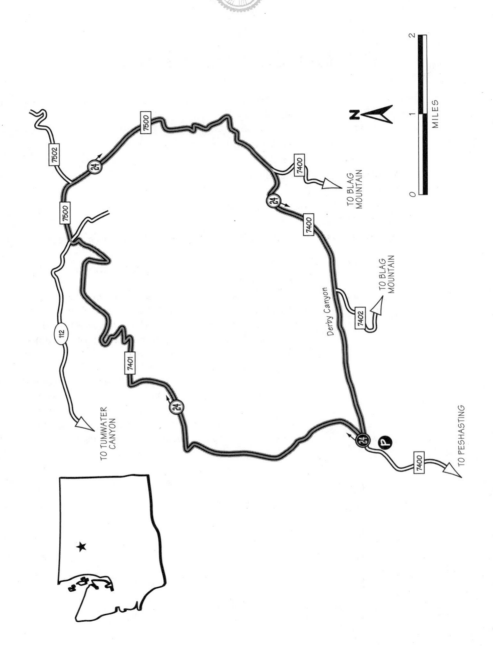

You can lead a "pony" to water . . .

Notes on the Trail

When you need to shake the lead out of your lederhosen after a visit to Leavenworth, head for the hills east of the Bavarian-themed town. Here's an opportunity to get your heart working while enjoying some pleasant scenery east of the rain curtain on Washington's drier side. This route is not singletrack but it does offer some of the best dirt-road riding around. The views are also outstanding. You won't likely see any vehicle traffic. However, there are flocks of sheep grazing in this area. This area is also popular with guided horse-back outfitters.

The Ride

0.0 Since there is no designated parking, mileage begins from the junction of FR 7400 and FR 7401. Keep left on FR 7401. Elevation 1,200 feet.

1.7 A gradual but persistent climb begins to get more steep. Tread is mostly packed dirt but with sandy sections and loose rocks.

3.3 You can begin to gain views of the Wenatchee River valley as you climb above the trees. Elevation 2,470 feet.

3.9 Cross behind the hills you've been climbing. You can now see north to distant snow-covered peaks. Elevation 2,795 feet.

4.5 Gulp down those views at 3,150 feet; they make the climb up satisfying, as well as the forthcoming descent. Watch for sections of sandy soil and loose rocks.

6.2 Elevation 2,545 feet.

8.3 After leveling out, the road descends some more. Elevation 2,290 feet.

9.0 Pass a Forest Service gate. Elevation 1,975 feet.

9.1 Junction. Turn right on FR 7500 and start climbing.

11.1 Still climbing. Elevation 2,640 feet.

12.1 The road is rutted and rough in places. Elevation 2,990 feet.

13.5 Back among the territorial views as you reach a four-way junction. Go right on the road that descends. This is the top of Derby Canyon, which makes for an almost illegally pleasurable descent.

14.5 Keep right as you pass the turnoff for the Blag Mountain Road. Keep descending on FR 7400.

16.6 Pass the other end of the road ascending Blag Mountain.

18.8 Back at junction of FR 7400 and FR 7401.

Interurban Flyer

Location:	6 miles south of Bellingham.
Distance:	6.8 miles, one way.
Tread:	Paved and gravel roads, packed gravel and dirt rail-trail.
Time:	2.5 to 3.5 hours.
Aerobic level:	Easy.
Technical difficulty:	1–2.
Best time to ride:	All year.
Facilities:	Toilets and water at Larrabee State Park.
Land status:	Bellingham Parks Department.
Maps:	DNR Map.
Access:	From Seattle, drive north on Interstate 5 for 63 miles. Take Washington Route 11 (Chuckanut Drive) north for approximately 14 miles. Park in a day-use parking lot on the right side just before Larrabee State Park. (From Bellingham, drive south on Chuckanut Drive.

NOTES ON THE TRAIL

Rail-trails make for near perfect introductions to mountain biking. They're also great for family outings, in which riders of differing abilities can amble along without having to worry too much about the steepness of the grade or the presence of cars. The former route of an interurban electric railway (which ran between Bellingham and Mount Vernon) offers a great no-hassles outing that has a bonus destination, the up and coming Fairhaven neighborhood of Bellingham. Ice cream, espresso, and baked goods are the ultimate motivators for bicyclists, right? And Fairhaven has them amid a charming red-brick ambience.

THE RIDE

0.0 The trail starts a few yards up Chuckanut Drive from the parking lot. Elevation 240 feet.

0.7 Cross a paved road. Elevation 325 feet.

1.4 Cross a valley once spanned by a trestle.

Interurban Flyer

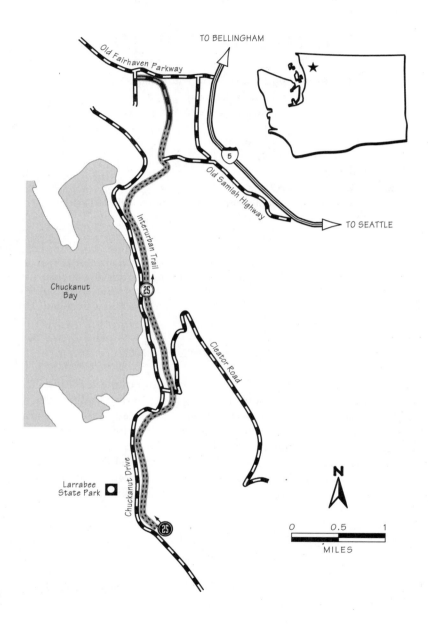

TO BELLINGHAM

Old Fairhaven Parkway

Old Samish Highway

5

TO SEATTLE

Interurban Trail

Chuckanut Bay

25

Cleator Road

Chuckanut Drive

Larrabee State Park

25

N

0   0.5   1

MILES

You'll catch glimpses of Puget Sound from parts of the Interurban Trail.

3.1 For the next 0.3 mile the trail also doubles as an entrance road to residents' homes. Watch for vehicles here.

4.1 Cross another valley by descending down one side and up the other. At the far side, the railroad grade goes through a cutting and then the trail veers off into a pleasant wooded valley. This section, which involves negotiating obstacles and steps, may prove difficult for beginners. Elevation 300 feet.

4.6 Cross a bridge and turn left.

4.7 Cross a busy road and proceed uphill to rejoin the interurban grade. This will be a walk for the majority of riders.

6.0 The grade is almost level and the trail almost straight as the urban fringe of Bellingham falls into view. The trail follows a short concrete section before resuming as dirt.

6.5 You'll see signs for Fairhaven. Keep descending, passing below a highway bridge.

6.8 At the sign for Padden Creek, turn right, then turn left on Donovan Avenue. This leads to Fairhaven's commercial area.

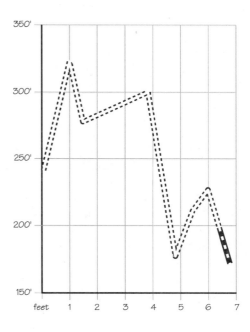

Walker Canyon Loop

Location:	7.5 miles northeast of Leavenworth, in the Wenatchee National Forest.
Distance:	16.2-mile loop.
Tread:	Dirt and gravel logging roads, some pavement.
Time:	2.5 to 3 hours.
Aerobic level:	Moderate.
Technical difficulty:	1–2.
Best time to ride:	April to October.
Facilities:	None.
Land status:	Wenatchee National Forest, Leavenworth Ranger District.
Maps:	Wenatchee National Forest, Leavenworth Ranger District.
Access:	Heading east from Leavenworth, turn left (north) onto Washington Route 209 (Chumstick Road) at the traffic light at the east end of town. (Don't cross the bridge on U.S. Highway 2 toward Wenatchee.) Drive 2.4 miles and turn right on Eagle Creek Road. Proceed up Eagle Creek for 1.4 miles to Forest Road 7510. There's not much space here, so park considerately at the edge of the forest road.

NOTES ON THE TRAIL

When the summer heat dissipates but before the soft glow of a Cascade sunset descends, pull on your shorts for a brisk ride to Walker Canyon. A series of canyons radiates from the Wenatchee River that carved its way through here. Logging roads extend for dozens of miles back into an uninhabited hinterland. You can customize many bike loops utilizing the roads that connect numerous canyons: This is but one that provides a good workout, some scenic views, and a healthy dose of solitude. After the descent, you'll even appreciate the pavement for the last 5.5 miles.

Walker Canyon Loop

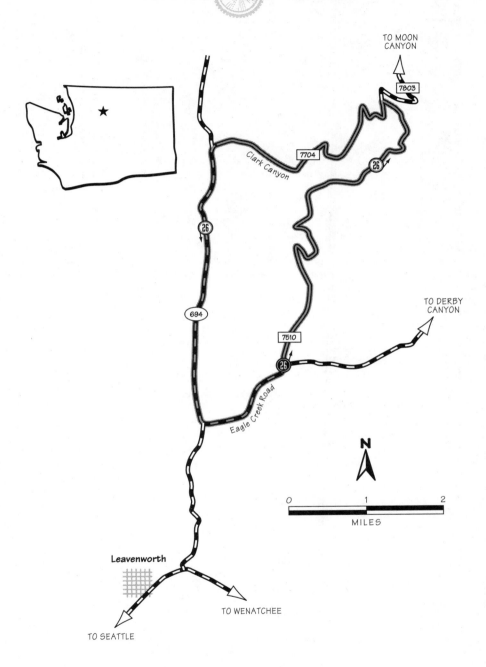

TO MOON
CANYON

7803

Clark Canyon

7704

26

26

TO DERBY
CANYON

694

7510

26

Eagle Creek Road

N

0   1   2

MILES

Leavenworth

TO WENATCHEE

TO SEATTLE

Walker Canyon makes for a great summer evening ride, when light floods the good dirt road that winds up hill.

THE RIDE

0.0   Ride up FR 7510. Elevation 1,515 feet.
2.0   Tread is pretty good: packed dirt mostly. Elevation 2,165 feet.
2.6   Climb eases off as you pass rock formations devised for a Hollywood Western. Elevation 2,370 feet.

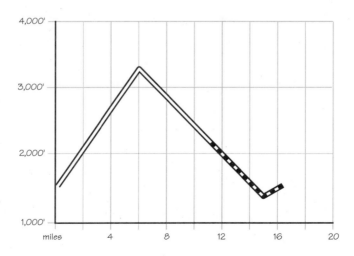

3.7 It's a long way down on the left side. Elevation 2,780 feet.

5.8 Elevation 3,270 feet.

6.0 Views to savor. Forest, mountains, and nary a house in sight.

6.3 Junction. FR 7510 ends here. Turn left onto FR 7704. (FR 7803 continues to the right.) This is the top of Clark Canyon and you ride to the bottom. It's a good road with loose gravel in places.

10.7 Enjoy the pleasures of the descent? The road loses about 400 feet of elevation per mile. Go left on the paved road (County Road 694).

14.8 Turn left on Eagle Creek Road.

16.2 Return to your vehicle.

Kitsap and Olympic Peninsulas

The long reach of Puget Sound separates most of the Kitsap and Olympic Peninsulas from the rest of the state, especially from the populous centers around Seattle. Hood Canal is the water boundary between the two peninsulas.

This is an area dominated by the Olympic Mountains, which often remain snow-dusted into the summer. Some of the toughest and most scenic rides in the state await those willing to head to the Olympics. Of course, riders can't pedal any of the inviting trails within the protected confines of Olympic National Park, but there are an additional 632,000 acres of Olympic National Forest that are open to mountain bikers.

There are several options for heading to the peninsulas: South Puget Sound riders have the choice of driving north across the Tacoma Narrows bridge; those living farther north must face a ferry ride. The ride itself is relaxing but the waiting time to get on a ferry in the summer months can be unpredictable. For that reason, many mountain bikers shun the big chunk of the state extending north from Gray's Harbor and west from Bainbridge Island. Here's a tip: Go midweek outside typical commute hours and the ferry lines are reasonable, even in the summer. Allow a half-hour before departure time and the chances are good that you'll get on board.

This chapter contains a representative selection of what's available on the west side of the water. There are a number of other rides possible by joining together loops using Forest Service roads. One thing to note about rides on the Olympic Peninsula is that because of the rugged terrain, hills can be extremely long and very steep. If you venture out to reconnoiter your own route, or to extend one written up here, check with a ranger station about road and trail conditions in advance. The peninsula gets bombarded by winter storms that tear up even the best-constructed thoroughfares.

Some of the rides closer to Puget Sound (such as Green Mountain near Bremerton) can be easily driven to and completed in a day. Those out and beyond Forks would be best undertaken over a weekend.

Early season conditions are often very wet, with slippery roots, rocks, and surface water. By July, even some of the wettest areas of the peninsula (which, after all, is home to the country's only temperate rain forest) should provide a dry tread.

For information on ferries, see the Appendix.

Dennie Ahl Loop

Location:	21 miles northwest of Shelton, in the Olympic National Forest.
Distance:	22.5 miles (full loop); 21.2 miles (out and back).
Tread:	Logging roads with packed dirt, packed gravel, and rough gravel.
Time:	3 to 5 hours.
Aerobic level:	Easy, with one tougher section to the summit.
Technical difficulty:	1–2; rough downhill section to complete the loop.
Best time to ride:	All year but best enjoyed when the roads are not wet.
Facilities:	USDA Forest Service campsite 8 miles from start.
Land status:	Olympic National Forest, Hood Canal Ranger District.
Maps:	Olympic National Forest, Hood Canal Ranger District; Green Trails Mount Tebo.
Access:	From Seattle, take a ferry to Bremerton and drive west on Washington Route 3. Just after the commercial strip in Belfair, turn right on WA 106 toward Union. Drive 18.7 miles along Hood Canal until the Purdy Cut-off Road. Go left and drive 2.8 miles farther until the intersection of U.S. Highway 101. Cross the highway. You'll see the George Adams Fish Hatchery on your right. Proceed up the Skokomish Valley Road for 5.7 miles until you reach the fork with Forest Road 23. Go right (uphill). The pavement changes to gravel after about a mile. Keep on FR 23 until you reach the junction with FR 2340. (You'll see signs for Dennie Ahl Seed Orchard.) Turn right and park after the initial uphill section. There's a level area on the left with some shade.

NOTES ON THE TRAIL

An investor might compare this ride to government bonds. The return won't match the profit from high-flying stocks but you won't lose your shirt either. The Dennie Ahl Loop offers a predictable ride over mostly well-groomed logging roads that rise gently up the hillside. The route is modest, which makes it ideally suited for a beginner. There's also a modest presence of other humans. So if you want a bit of solitude and an enjoyable, none-too-demanding wander in the woods, head over to the westside of Hood Canal.

Dennie Ahl Loop

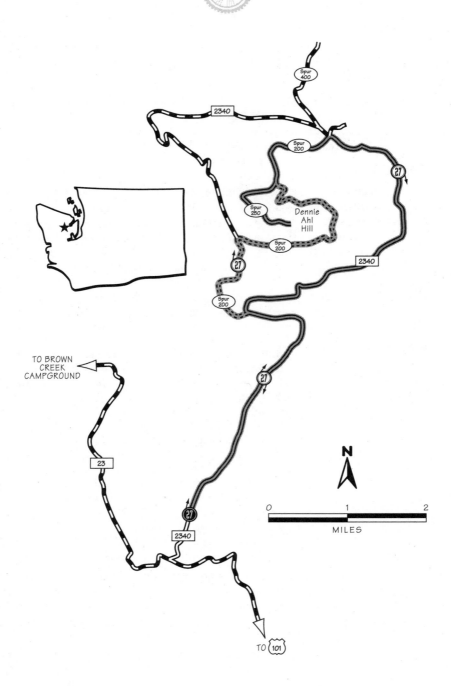

Spur 400

2340

Spur 200

27

Spur 250

Dennie Ahl Hill

Spur 200

27

2340

Spur 200

TO BROWN CREEK CAMPGROUND

23

27

N

27

2340

TO (101)

0   1   2
MILES

Speaking of which, you'll get a peek-a-boo view of the canal's Great Bend and the Skokomish Delta from the summit. Fast-growing Douglas-firs block most of the view of the Olympic Mountains to the west. Although this can be ridden as a loop, retracing your tire marks offers a less bumpy and brake-wrenching descent. The out-and-back route is recommended for beginners.

THE RIDE

0.0 From the unofficial trailhead, go left on FR 2340. Elevation 530 feet.

1.0 Pass through a clear-cut area.

2.2 Cross the high steel bridge and marvel at the Skokomish River gorge several hundred feet below. Elevation 550 feet.

3.1 Road forks. Keep left. The gated road leads to the seed orchard.

4.4 Three-way road junction. The main road bends to the right; a rough road goes straight; you keep left on spur road 200. It's marked with a small brown sign. Elevation 615 feet. Let the gradual climbing begin.

5.7 Spur road 210. Keep straight. Elevation 830 feet.

6.0 Spur road 230. Keep straight. Road surface smoothes out as you climb between strands of second-growth Douglas-firs.

6.5 Elevation 1,000 feet.

7.0 Elevation 1,130 feet.

7.3 Short respite from the climb as you dip and round a bend.

8.0 Elevation 1,320 feet.

9.2 Junction with spur road 250. Elevation 1,460 feet. Go left and begin the brisk climb to the summit. This is probably the hardest part of the ride.

10.6 Reach summit, elevation 2,004.

12.0 Return to junction with spur road 200.

Note: Beyond this junction, you have a choice of how you return. The smoother route is back the way you came. To head back the way you came, simply turn right at the bottom of spur road 250. For the loop-inclined, follow these instructions:

12.0 Go left at the foot of spur road 250.

12.3 Spur road 290. Keep right as the descent gets serious. Be prepared for loose rocks and mounded gravel on the corners.

13.0 More rocks as the road plummets downhill.

13.3 Junction with FR 2340. Go right. Elevation 1,165 feet.

14.0 Pass evidence of a landslide and feel the result of the road's regrade.

14.2 Three-way intersection. Keep right on FR 2340.

14.6 Pass another unnumbered spur road.

15.1 Pass a spur road with old numbering (8700).

15.5 Another spur slips by as the road levels out.

15.9 Enter a clear-cut area.

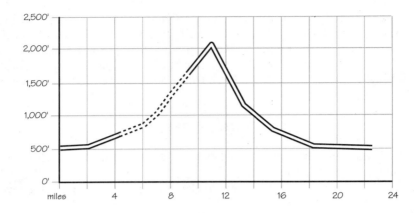

17.4 As you enter another clearing, the continuation of the road on the other side of the valley is visible.

18.1 Pass spur road 200, where you turned off a couple of hours earlier.

20.1 Back to the high bridge, but there's always time to stop and admire the view again.

22.5 Your car is waiting in the shade.

Foothills Loop

Location:	2.5 miles south of Port Angeles.
Distance:	17.1-mile loop.
Tread:	Paved road, dirt singletrack, and gravel road.
Time:	3 to 4 hours.
Aerobic level:	Strenuous.
Technical difficulty:	4.
Best time to ride:	June to October.
Facilities:	Toilets and water at Olympic National Park visitors' center.
Land status:	DNR.
Maps:	Custom Correct Hurricane Ridge.
Access:	From Seattle, take a ferry across Puget Sound and follow Washington Route 104 and then U.S. Highway 101 to Port Angeles. Turn left on Race Street. Drive 0.6 mile to the Olympic National Park visitor center and park.

Notes on the trail

Since bikes aren't allowed on trails within national parks, this is as close as you can legally get to riding in Olympic National Park. Besides, most of the trails in the park are too steep for bikes anyway. You can gain a sampling of the terrain by taking this loop through the Foothills, a range of hills that lies between the city of Port Angeles and the brooding peaks of the park. Once you're on the trail proper, you can zip along through a thinned forest that gets a reasonable amount of light. But be warned, this is a physically demanding ride. Heavy motorcycle use has eroded deep ruts in the trail, making it advisable to avoid after rains.

The Ride

0.0 Start at the visitor center parking lot and exit right and uphill. Almost immediately, keep left at the intersection and onto Mount Angeles Road (i.e., not the main road into the park). Elevation 285 feet.

1.5 Elevation 657 feet.

2.5 Just beyond a sign for Walking Horse Hill, turn right onto a gated dirt road. Go around the gate. You begin on a decrepit logging road that is being reclaimed by nature.

Foothills Loop

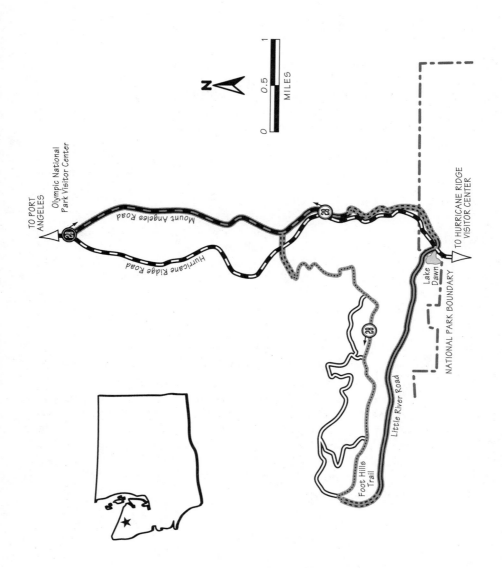

Don't be fooled. When it rains here, expect lots of deep puddles.

2.6 Cross a bridge above the main road into the park. Elevation 1,391 feet.

4.3 Junction, keep right. The road gets rougher and steeper here. Elevation 1,875 feet.

5.0 Watch for trail starting in the woods on your right. Turn onto the trail, which is rutted in numerous places. Elevation 2,430 feet.

5.6 Trail junction. Keep left. Elevation 2,520 feet.

6.5 Junction. Keep left. Elevation 2,250 feet.

7.7 Junction. Keep left. Elevation 2,205 feet.

8.6 Exit the narrow comfort of the singletrack onto the main access road used by motorcyclists. Turn left and proceed downhill on the gravel road. Elevation 1,725 feet.

9.0 Junction with Little River Road. Elevation 1,390 feet. Turn left (uphill).

11.0 Road changes from dirt to pavement. Elevation 1,841 feet.

12.2 Junction with Hurricane Ridge Road. Elevation 1,795 feet. Proceed straight across and behind gate. Walk your bike on the right of the gravel piles. In about 100 yards you're on an abandoned paved road.

12.9 Cross behind boulder placed in center of road; watch for broken glass here.

13.3 The traffic you hear is on the main road into the national park. You get views out to the Strait of Juan de Fuca from here.

13.5 After a brief uphill, you reach the gated lower end of this old road. Walk around the gate. The pavement resumes here. Elevation 1,305 feet.

17.1 Proceed downhill and retrace your route back to the visitors' center.

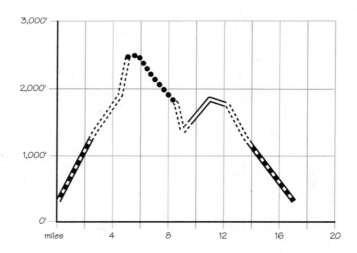

Gold Creek Loop

Location:	15 miles southeast of Sequim, in the Olympic National Forest.
Distance:	19.3-mile loop.
Tread:	Gravel logging road, singletrack.
Time:	4 to 5 hours.
Aerobic level:	3. Moderate to Strenuous.
Technical difficulty:	4–5. Skilled.
Best time to ride:	May to October.
Facilities:	None.
Land status:	Olympic National Forest, Quilcene Ranger District.
Maps:	Olympic National Forest, Quilcene Ranger District.
Access:	From Seattle, take either the Bainbridge Island or Edmonds ferry. Cross the Hood Canal Bridge and follow Washington Route 104 to U.S. Highway 101 in the direction of Sequim and Port Angeles. Just before Sequim Bay State Park, turn left on Louella Road. Follow it to a T-junction and turn left on Palo Alto Road, which turns from pavement to gravel. Drive it for 5.4 miles until the Y-junction with Forest Road 28 and FR 2880. Bear left and then turn right on FR 2860. Follow it for approximately 3 miles, past the East Crossing Campground. Park just before the bridge at the Gold Creek Trailhead.

NOTES ON THE TRAIL

Don't underestimate this trail or overestimate your abilities. It will test your limits of handling skills and punish you severely for a mistake. This trail has a narrow tread in places and potentially dangerous drop-offs. Only experienced riders should consider tackling it. OK, the lecture's over. If you think you're ready for this ride, you're in for some highly challenging but satisfying miles. Sure, there are pleasing views of the Dungeness River Valley but if you're coming here, come strictly for the riding experience. Besides, gawking at the scenery might be detrimental to your health when you finally make it onto the singletrack. Note: As this guidebook went to press, rangers reported severe winter damage in 1998-99 on the access roads to Gold Creek. Call ahead to the Quilcene Ranger Station to confirm access before driving out there. See the Appendix for phone number.

Gold Creek

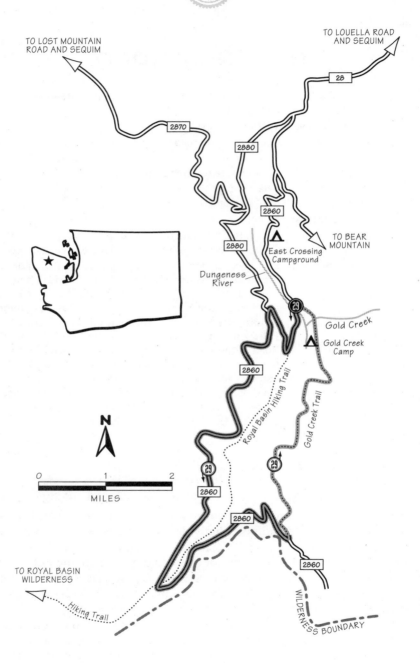

TO LOST MOUNTAIN
ROAD AND SEQUIM

TO LOUELLA ROAD
AND SEQUIM

28

2870

2880

2860

2880

East Crossing
Campground

TO BEAR
MOUNTAIN

Dungeness
River

29

Gold Creek

Gold Creek
Camp

Royal Basin Hiking Trail

Gold Creek Trail

2860

N

0   1   2
MILES

29

2860

29

2860

2860

TO ROYAL BASIN
WILDERNESS

Hiking Trail

WILDERNESS BOUNDARY

You're never far from water on many parts of the Olympic Peninsula.

THE RIDE

0.0 Cross the river and head uphill on FR 2860. Elevation 1,547 feet.

1.0 The gravel logging road curves back as you continue to climb steeply.

1.9 Junction with FR 2880. Keep left on FR 2860.

3.6 First real glimpse of the steeply sided valley.

3.7 Climbing peaks at 2,570 feet.

4.5 Begin a long descent toward the trailhead used by backpackers heading to the Royal Basin in Olympic National Park or Buckhorn Wilderness in Olympic National Forest.

8.7 Royal Basin Trailhead. Stay on FR 2860. Elevation 1,915 feet.

10.0 Start climbing again.

11.3 Cross bridge over Copper Creek.

12.5 Gold Creek Trailhead is on your left. Let the real ride begin.

13.8 Roll along on soft forest floor. Look left to see FR 2860 you descended on the other side of the valley.

14.6 Trail narrows to barely the width of the helmet clamped on your noggin. If you want to admire the precipitous edge, stop first.

14.7 Trail starts to climb.

15.3 Watch for the loose rocks as you climb.

16.3 Keep left and head downhill at this junction.

17.0 This is what free-falling is like.

17.3 First of a series of switchbacks as you continue to lose altitude. Gravity will shortly be against you as you begin a short climb. This section of trail has been repaired recently with gravel, which adds to the challenge.

19.0 Open area next to the creek is the campsite. Ford Gold Creek here and follow the trail briefly uphill.

19.3 Feel a sense of accomplishment as you reach FR 2860.

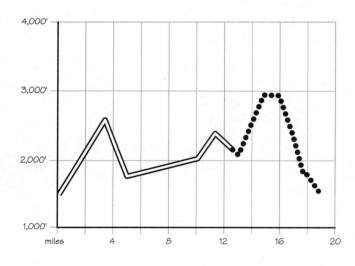

Howell Lake Loop

Location:	10.5 miles northwest of Belfair, in the Tahuya State Forest.
Distance:	7.4-mile loop.
Tread:	Dirt singletrack with loose gravel, sandy in places.
Time:	1 to 1.5 hours.
Aerobic level:	Moderate. Some short, steep hills and lots of small ups and downs.
Technical difficulty:	2–4. Challenging in places, with loose rocks, roots, sandy soil, and steep hills.
Best time to ride:	Open from April 15 to October 15.
Facilities:	Primitive camping; vault toilets at trailhead.
Land status:	DNR Tahuya State Forest.
Maps:	DNR Tahuya State Forest.
Access:	From Seattle, take a ferry to Bremerton and follow Washington Route 3 west to Belfair. Turn right on the Old Belfair Highway and then left on WA 300 (at the corner with the QFC supermarket) for approximately 3 miles. Turn right on the Belfair-Tahuya Road and drive uphill for 4 miles until a sign for the Lake Howell Campground. Go left for an additional 1.6 miles until the entrance to the campsite. Park there.

NOTES ON THE TRAIL

This is one of a number of offroad vehicle (ORV) areas owned and operated by the Washington Department of Natural Resources. Expect to see lots of motorcycles and ATVs on the weekends, but come midweek you'll practically have the trails to yourself. There are many miles of trails here but some have seen regular motorcycle use and are therefore in poor shape. The Lake Howell Loop is a great excuse for some rip-roaring fun. The area is mostly flat with no hills of any consequence. But plentiful short, steep sections test the mettle of your technical skill. There are sections that can be thoroughly enjoyed by an energetic beginner wishing to enhance riding skills, but otherwise it's not recommended for neophytes. Trails are also open to equestrians and hikers.

Howell Lake Loop

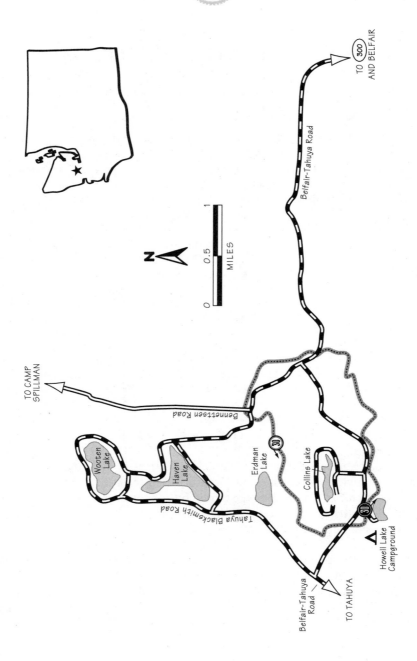

TO 300 AND BELFAIR

Belfair-Tahuya Road

N

MILES
0   0.5   1

TO CAMP SPILLMAN

Bennettsen Road

Wooten Lake

Haven Lake

Erdman Lake

Tahuya Blacksmith Road

Collins Lake

Howell Lake Campground

Belfair-Tahuya Road

TO TAHUYA

THE RIDE

0.0 Start at campsite, follow sign for Camp Spillman, 7.7 miles.

0.5 First steep section.

1.0 Trail briefly parallels road you drove in on.

1.8 Drop through a pretty green gully with lots of ferns. Tread transitions to dirt.

2.1 Steep descent with tree roots, loose river rocks.

2.3 Enter a clear-cut area. Sandy soil.

2.7 Re-enter the woods.

2.8 Cross the Belfair-Tahuya Road.

3.2 Enjoy a smooth section of whoop-de-doo hills.

4.2 Come to a junction. Keep left.

4.3 Cross Bennettsen Road (gravel).

4.4 Cross Belfair-Tahuya Road.

4.6 Cross handsome iron bridge.

5.0 Meander through salal and fern-covered forest.

5.4 Prepare for steep uphill.

6.1 Enter area of new-growth Douglas-fir forest.

6.9 Steep section before crossing Belfair-Tahuya Road.

7.4 Exit on to gravel road at campsite.

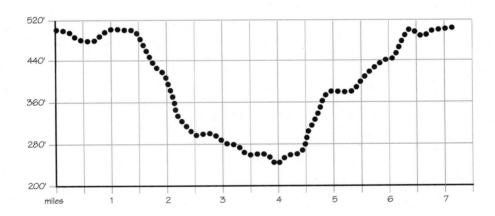

Lower Big Quilcene

Location:	5.4 miles west of Quilcene, in the Olympic National Forest.
Distance:	12.4 miles, out and back.
Tread:	Singletrack.
Time:	2.5 to 3.5 hours.
Aerobic level:	2. Moderate.
Technical difficulty:	1–4; starts easy but exposed roots, rocks, and other obstacles quickly demand experienced to skilled rider skills.
Best time to ride:	April to October.
Facilities:	Primitive toilet at trailhead; camping nearby.
Land status:	Olympic National Forest, Quilcene Ranger District.
Maps:	Olympic National Forest, Quilcene Ranger District.
Access:	From Seattle, cross Puget Sound by ferry and follow Washington Route 104 for 13 miles in the direction of Port Angeles. Turn south on U.S. Highway 101 for 9 miles to Quilcene and drive through it. Just under a mile beyond the Quilcene Ranger Station, take a right onto Penny Creek Road. Take the left fork onto Big Quilcene River Road (Forest Road 2740) and proceed uphill on the paved road for 4.5 miles. Stay on the pavement until you see the trailhead sign. Turn left on the short gravel road that leads down to the parking lot.

NOTES ON THE TRAIL

Seasoned hikers often remark that distances in the Olympic Mountains are misleading because the terrain is so tough. That applies to bike rides, too. This ride has the added complication that it starts out gently, lulls you into thinking it will be a quick and pleasant experience, and then reveals its true self: a tough little trail. Definitely a good workout for the legs and lungs, as well as the brain. The latter needs to be firing on all synapses for quick thinking on the best route to avoid a root, a rock, or a tricky section of trail. What you get in return is a forest that even Hollywood couldn't invent. Its flora ranges from hanging moss to gnarly Pacific yews and towering Douglas-firs.

Lower Big Quilcene

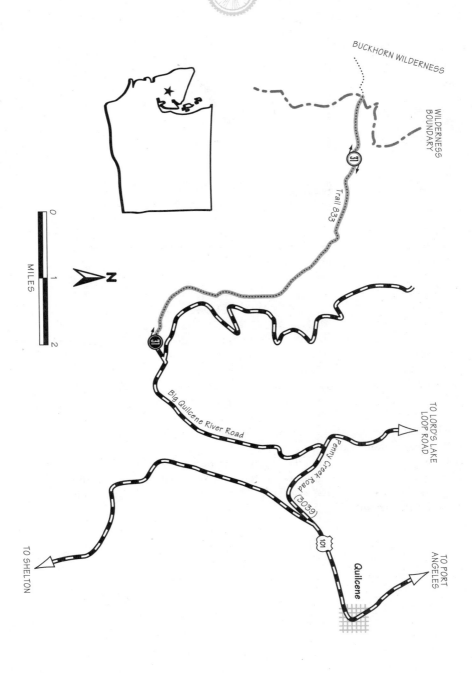

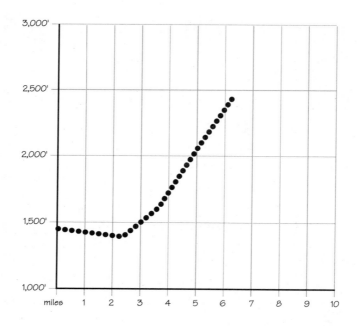

THE RIDE

0.0 Lower Big Quilcene Trailhead (sign indicates distance to Trail 2750). Elevation approximately 1,500 feet.

1.6 The first of numerous wooden bridges.

2.4 Bridge over the Lower Quilcene River. Elevation 1,455 feet.

4.4 Series of downed firs that have been cut to allow passage.

4.5 Trail zips up and down at will.

4.6 Narrow section that is subject to landslides.

4.8 Steep uphill section.

5.1 Ford a stream that in early summer can be up to 20 feet wide.

6.2 After a tough final mile, reach the turnaround at the edge of the Buckhorn Wilderness. Elevation 2,400 feet. Turn around at the shelter and head back.

12.4 Back at trailhead.

Lower South Fork Skokomish

Location:	22 miles northwest of Shelton, in the Olympic National Forest.
Distance:	20.8-mile loop.
Tread:	Singletrack (varies from excellent to muddy and rough with roots and gravel), gravel logging road, some pavement.
Time:	5 hours.
Aerobic level:	Moderate to strenuous.
Technical difficulty:	4–5. Note: River to ford.
Best time to ride:	Mid-June to late September.
Facilities:	Camping at Brown Campsite close to trailhead.
Land status:	Olympic National Forest, Hood Canal Ranger District.
Maps:	Olympic National Forest, Hood Canal Ranger District; Green Trails Mount Tebo.
Access:	From Seattle, take a ferry to Bremerton and follow Washington Route 3 to Belfair. At the edge of town, turn right on WA 106 toward Union. Drive 18.7 miles along Hood Canal until the Purdy Cut-off Road. Go left and drive 2.8 miles to the intersection of U.S. Highway 101. Cross the highway. You'll see the George Adams Fish Hatchery on your right. Proceed up the Skokomish Valley Road until you reach the fork with Forest Road 23. Go right (uphill). The pavement changes to gravel after about a mile but again becomes paved for the remaining 9 miles to the signed trailhead.

NOTES ON THE TRAIL

Pack your sense of adventure for this one. There are steep ups and downs, narrow log bridges, boggy sections, scenery, and more. Oh, yes, and a river to ford. This is the type of trail that will be good for a story or two. The best part may be that it doesn't get much bike traffic. That's partly because storm damage closed the trail for several seasons and even now it's not in ideal condition. That said, it's a good ride for honing your handling skills but won't tax you mile after mile. Since there's a horse camp nearby expect to see equestrians during weekends on the trail's first six miles or so. Pick a warm day so that you don't get chilled after crossing the river. Bring a pair of river runner shoes if you don't want to get your cycling shoes wet.

Lower South Fork Skokomish

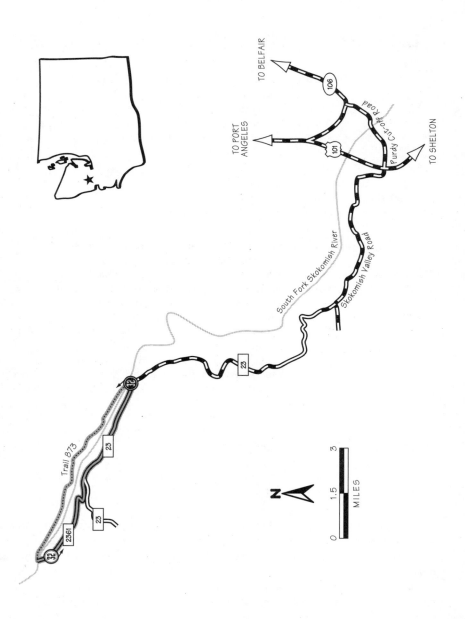

TO BELFAIR

TO PORT ANGELES

TO SHELTON

106

101

Purdy Cut-off Road

South Fork Skokomish River

Skokomish Valley Road

23

32

Trail 873

23

2361

23

32

N

MILES

0   1.5   3

It's an easy cruise back to the trailhead on this part of the Lower South Fork Skokomish ride.

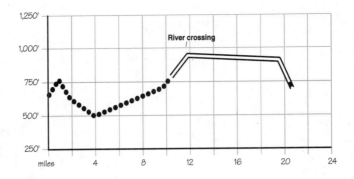

THE RIDE

0.0 Trailhead elevation 580 feet.

0.2 Good tread for traction as you grunt up this first steep section, which clings to the hillside.

0.3 Unmarked fork. Keep left.

0.4 Top out (momentarily) and marvel at the giant Douglas-firs.

0.8 Drop down toward the river. Steep and rough in places.

1.0 Cross stream. Muddy and slippery.

1.3 Get a close up view of the Skokomish as you ride on a raised bar of gravel.

1.7 Another stream where you'll see evidence of equine feet.

1.9 Two wooden walkways.

2.0 Bridge.

2.1 Attractive open area that seems to say "you must rest here."

2.6 Trail rolls along valley floor and then you hit an uphill, the first of many to come.

3.5 More ups and downs and bridges to cross.

4.4 Pleasant view of the river as you cross another bridge.

5.4 Trail climbs sharply to avoid a landslide area that occurred in the winter of 1994–1995.

5.9 Swoosh through a younger forest as the trail dives back down to the river.

7.0 Rough section with rocks and mud.

7.3 Cross a narrow stream.

7.8 Give a nod of thanks to the crews who cleared the storm-downed trees that litter this area.

8.5 Trail climbs briefly. Watch out for roots, rocks, and mud.

8.8 Look for sign saying "Harp's Shelter 1.5 miles". The current section of trail ends soon after here at a bridge that dangles diving-board style over the Skokomish. Keep to the right before the bridge and follow the rough trail that goes away from the river.

9.5 Sign for horses' ford. Keep on the trail.

9.6 Narrow log bridge (first of two) that requires you to carry your bike.

10.0 Descend down to meet the river. The log bridge across the Skokomish is unsafe and closed to everyone. Not to worry. Double back on the trail about 50 feet and scramble down the embankment to a pebbly area at the first visible bend. Wear some kind of shoes to cross the river. It's cold and full of sharp rocks. You won't cross it successfully in your bare feet. In early summer, the water level is about calf-high. Once across, retrace your route to the bridge and pick up the trail again.

10.3 Trail pops out on FR 2361. Go left and follow this largely level gravel logging road for another five miles. This road is wide and because of the trees there are no views.

15.3 Junction with FR 23. Go straight. (Spider Lake is 4 miles to the right.) As you can tell, this section is simply to complete the loop.

18.8 At last, the road starts to descend seriously.

19.9 Pull on the brakes for the sharp left turn to the trailhead road. Signed Brown Creek Campground. This part is paved.

20.5 Cross bridge and immediately turn left toward the trailhead.

20.8 You're back at the trailhead.

33

Mount Muller

Location: 24 miles east of Forks in the Olympic National Forest.
Distance: 13.5-mile loop.
Tread: Singletrack, rough in places; some doubletrack logging road.
Time: 4.5 to 5 hours.
Aerobic level: Strenuous.
Technical difficulty: 4–5.
Best time to ride: June to September.
Facilities: Vault toilet at trailhead.
Land status: Olympic National Forest, Soleduck Ranger District; DNR.
Maps: Olympic National Forest, Soleduck Ranger District; Green Trails, Pysht.
Access: From Port Angeles, drive west on U.S. Highway 101 toward Forks. Look for an electrical sub-station on the right just before milepost 216. Turn right and drive the half-mile to the trailhead.

NOTES ON THE TRAIL

This is a tough ride that's physically demanding on the way up and techni-cally demanding once you get to the top. In exchange for heaving lungs and straining calves you can, if the fickle weather cooperates, receive outstand-ing views across the Strait of Juan de Fuca, Mount Olympus and Mount Crescent. You'll also ride through several high meadows and get a sampling of what life was like for Mount Muller lookout operators. For technical aficionados who can't resist jumping wayward logs, there are lots of rocks, roots, and debris to practice on here as you climb up and descend the ridge that stretches 4.5 miles along the top. It's not all hardship. The final descent is 5 miles of exhilaration through the woods. This is where you should look out for other trail users, since up until this point your speed barely exceeds that of a hiker. Be prepared for low altitude clouds that make the top brisk on even hot days.

Mount Muller and Rock House

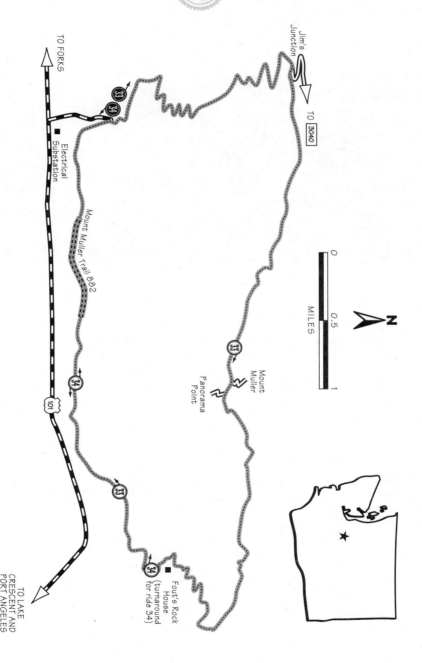

TO FORKS

Jimi's Junction

TO 3040

33
34

Electrical Substation

Mount Muller Trail 882

34

101

33

Panorama Point

Mount Muller

33

34

Fout's Rock House (turnaround for ride 34)

TO LAKE CRESCENT AND PORT ANGELES

MILES
0   0.5   1

N

Looking across to the Olympic range from the Mount Muller Trail.

THE RIDE

0.0 From the trailhead, ride east briefly and then turn north away from the main trail. Elevation 1,000 feet.

0.5 There's tree shade and salal by the trailside. Elevation 1,195 feet.

0.6 "Miners Crossing" indicates old mining road. Elevation 1,285 feet.

1.0 Smooth dirt tread won't impede you. Elevation 1,585 feet.

1.6 Elevation 2,130 feet.

2.0 Start traversing the side of the hill again. Elevation 2,360 feet.

2.5 Forest still has lots of shade for a warm day. Just ahead is a sign indicating "Nosebag Point." Elevation 2,745 feet.

2.9 Leave the woods and enter Grouse Meadow. Elevation 3,025 feet.

3.0 Above the trees at last. Views south to the Sol Duc Valley and the snowy Olympic peaks. Elevation 3,085 feet.

3.2 Jim's Junction. Elevation 3,170 feet. Turn right.

3.5 Ride initially along a narrow ridge, then sidehill through Millsap Meadow. Elevation 3,530 feet.

3.7 Trail descends briefly to 3,200 feet as you enter an area of skinny trees.

4.0 View of strait and Vancouver Island. (Note that parts of the trail are often immersed in low clouds.)

4.3 Thomas Gap. Elevation 3,000 feet.

4.6 A series of steep switchbacks with rocks and other obstacles.

4.9 Jasmine Meadow. Elevation 3,375 feet.

5.3 More ups and downs as you make your way along the ridge. Elevation 3,415 feet.

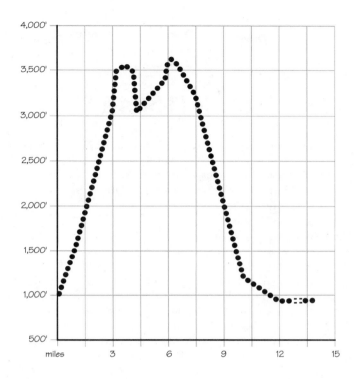

5.7 Junction for the top of Mount Muller. Views north are limited because of trees. It's a four-minute walk to the top. Keep right for the descent. Elevation 3,635 feet.

5.8 Great views eastward toward Lake Crescent.

6.2 The trail alternates between the north and south side of the ridge for a footholding. Elevation 3,465 feet.

6.7 Trail descends briefly. Elevation 3,295 feet.

7.1 Elevation 3,165 feet.

7.2 Elevation 3,200 feet.

8.2 The tread has smoothed out as the trail winds down the hill. Elevation 2,530 feet. A rapid descent awaits you over the next 2 miles.

10.2 Elevation 1,200 feet.

11.0 The descent is over. A series of ups and downs follows as you ride through the forest of the valley floor.

12.2 Trail joins an old logging road. Keep right. Elevation 960 feet.

13.0 More gentle ups and down. Elevation 950 feet.

13.5 Back to trailhead.

Rock House

See Map
on Page 141

Location: 24 miles east of Forks, in the Olympic National Forest.

Distance: 6.6 miles, out and back.

Tread: Singletrack, some doubletrack.

Time: 1.5 to 2.5 hours.

Aerobic level: Easy.

Technical difficulty: 1.

Best time to ride: April to October.

Facilities: Vault toilet at trailhead.

Land status: Olympic National Forest, Soleduck Ranger District; DNR.

Maps: Olympic National Forest, Soleduck Ranger District; Green Trails, Pysht.

Access: From Port Angeles, drive west toward Forks on U.S. Highway 101. Look for an electrical sub-station on the right just before milepost 216. Turn right and drive the half-mile to the trailhead.

NOTES ON THE TRAIL

If you're not up to the gruesome climbing required to ascend Mount Muller, this ride makes for the perfect alternative. It has almost no climbing yet contains lots of interesting swoops and turns as you wind through the forest floor. There are a few bumps and small obstacles but mostly you'll be rolling on naturally mulched forest, with some river gravel thrown in occasionally. Makes for a great outing for a beginner willing to test handling skills. I set the turnaround point at 3.3 miles, which

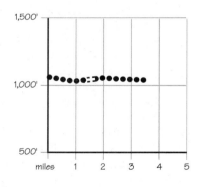

is when the trail begins to steepen. If you're up for it, press on to Fout's Rock House, an unmistakably large boulder next to the trail. Getting there involves a wee bit of climbing. Progressing farther still presents increasingly tougher inclines.

THE RIDE

0.0 Leave the trailhead heading east. Elevation 1,000 feet.

0.5 Trail invitingly wanders through an airy forest. Elevation 950 feet.

1.0 Trail merges here. Keep right as the trail widens into an old logging road.

1.3 Road narrows back down to singletrack as it rolls along the forest floor. Elevation 960 feet.

2.0 It's hard not to have fun as the narrow trail whips up and down and around. Elevation 970 feet.

2.5 There's a series of small ups and downs to prepare you for the start of climbing. Elevation 975 feet. Get ready for the climb to begin in earnest.

3.0 Elevation 1,100 feet.

3.3 Anywhere in the next half-mile is a good turnaround if you don't want to face the climb. Elevation 1,200 feet. Beyond here the trail gains elevation at the rate of about 600 feet per mile. Fout's Rock House is another mile uphill from here.

Quinault Ridge

Location:	5 miles south of Lake Quinault, in the Olympic National Forest.
Distance:	17.1 miles, out and back.
Tread:	Good, packed gravel road.
Time:	3 to 3.5 hours.
Aerobic level:	Moderate.
Technical difficulty:	1–2.
Best time to ride:	Year-round.
Facilities:	None; campgrounds on the shores of Lake Quinault to the north.
Land status:	Olympic National Forest, Quinault Ranger District.
Maps:	Olympic National Forest, Quinault Ranger District.
Access:	From Seattle, head south 63 miles on Interstate 5 to Washington Route 8, south of Olympia. Drive west on U.S. Highway 101 and WA 12 toward Aberdeen. Then go north on WA 8 and US 101 for approximately 53 miles. Turn right onto Forest Road 2258, which is located between mileposts 118 and 119 on US 101. Park close to the intersection with US 101.

Notes on the Trail

The Quinault Ranger District of the Olympic National Forest wants to encourage mountain biking. So far, the district has limited offerings but with support and encouragement from riders is willing to explore expanding the selection of rides. This ride is an undemanding out-and-back that could become part of a pleasing loop that would drop down toward Lake Quinault. The district abounds with other loop possibilities, joining a logging road here to one over there. Let the Forest Service staff know there's interest by visiting and riding here. This route gives you a flavor of what this area offers—scenic views across forest and lake, with glimpses of the Pacific thrown in. You can add an extra 15 miles by riding beyond the gate at the top of the hill to the end of the road. This particular section of road is due to be decommissioned; leaving it free of motor vehicles.

Quinault Ridge

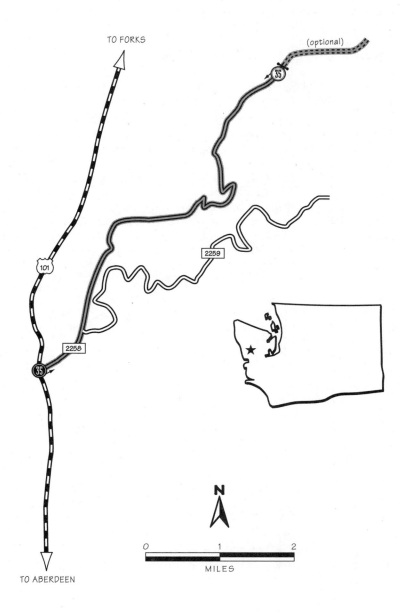

TO FORKS

(optional)

35

101

2259

2258

35

TO ABERDEEN

N

0   1   2

MILES

THE RIDE

0.0 Head up FR 2258 away from US 101. Elevation 445 feet.

0.8 Junction. Keep left on 2258. Watch for truck traffic mid-week. Elevation 680 feet.

1.5 Climb up through second-growth forest on a good single-lane road. Elevation 865 feet.

3.0 You can hear stream noise as you ride among pleasant forest. Elevation 980 feet.

3.5 Road gets steeper. Elevation 1,055 feet.

4.0 A mixture of cedar, pine, fir, and alder as the road levels off at 1,240 feet.

4.5 Trees block the view for the moment. Elevation 1,400 feet.

5.0 Views in both directions across the Quinault Ridge. Elevation 1,605 feet.

6.0 More views to the east toward the Colonel Bob Wilderness. Elevation 2,125 feet.

7.1 Views keep getting better. Now you can see toward Amanda Park. Elevation 2,315 feet.

7.5 Reach gate. The road beyond is closed to motor vehicles for habitat protection. Go around gate onto partially grassed-over road. Elevation 2,390 feet.

8.5 The road clings to a hillside and descends into the valley for another 3 miles before ending. If the weather is clear, you can see where the road ends. If you don't mind hauling back up the hill, ride on to where the road ends, 6.5 miles farther on. Or turn around here at the 1-mile marker. Elevation 2,320 feet.

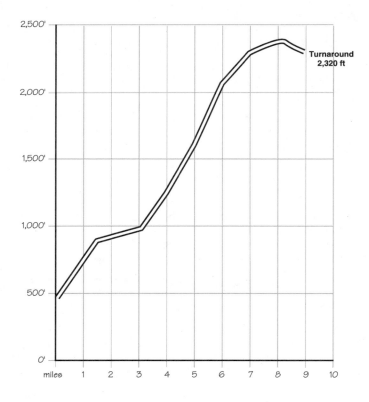

On a clear day you can see Lake Crescent and the coast from the Quinault Ridge Trail.

9.5 Back to gate. Let the descent begin.

15.3 You can glimpse the ocean in the distance as you whiz downhill.

16.3 Pass the end of FR 2259. Elevation 700 feet.

17.1 Back to your vehicle.

Wildcat Loop

Location:	Green Mountain State Forest, 7 miles northwest of Bremerton.
Distance:	11.3-mile loop.
Tread:	Mainly singletrack with short sections of gravel road.
Time:	2.5 to 3 hours.
Aerobic level:	Moderate.
Technical difficulty:	2–4.
Best time to ride:	Open all year but not advised after heavy rains.
Facilities:	Camping, vault toilet at trailhead, water at the campsite.
Land status:	DNR Green Mountain State Forest.
Maps:	USGS Wildcat Lake; DNR Green Mountain.
Access:	From the Seattle area, go west from the Bainbridge Island and Kingston ferries to Washington Route 3. Exit at NW Anderson Hill Road and proceed west for 3 miles. Turn left at the junction (Chevron gas station) with Seabeck Highway NW. Go south 3.75 miles until NW Holly Road. Turn right and proceed west again for another 1.8 miles. Watch for the Wildcat Trailhead parking lot on your left.

NOTES ON THE TRAIL

A great all-round trail ride with lots of singletrack, some challenging sections, and memorable views of the Seattle skyline, some 15 miles to the east. It's a tough slog to the top, with only a few brief moments of roller-coaster before you are again pounding the pedals but the views more than compensate. Since it's uphill to the summit, the trip back to the parking lot is virtually a free ride. The last 1.5 miles is one of the best sections of any trail this side of the Methow Valley. Undiluted fun for those willing to test their handling mettle. The trail can be enjoyed year-round, although to halt erosion it's best to stay away after heavy rains. Since this is a working forest you may occasionally find trail detours to accommodate logging activities.

Wildcat Loop

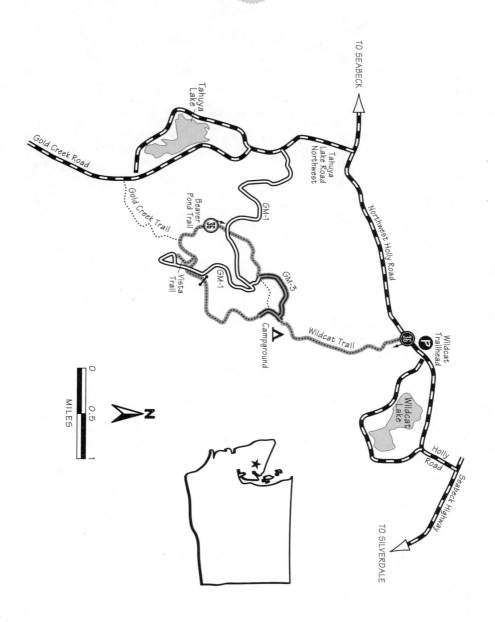

There are plenty of opportunities to exercise your brakes on the Wildcat downhills.

THE RIDE

0.0 Head uphill from the parking lot. Elevation 500 feet.

0.3 Enjoy great views of the forest on a brief roller-coaster.

1.0 Cross a gravel logging road, follow trail directly ahead. Elevation 610 feet.

1.3 Elevation 860 feet.

1.4 Descend to a dirt road and cross it diagonally to pick up the trail.

1.7 Cross another road. Elevation 910 feet.

2.1 After another short, steeper section, emerge onto another road. Turn left toward the campground. Elevation 1,135 feet. (This extends the ride and avoids a particularly steep section of the trail.)

2.2 Pass through the campground and turn right onto the trail between the rail fence. Elevation 1,155 feet.

2.5 Admire the rhododendrons as you negotiate imbedded rocks on the trail. Elevation 1,200 feet

3.1 Brief uphill and begin to round the shoulder of the mountain. Elevation 1,390 feet.

3.7 At the bottom of the hill, turn right at the road and then a quick left back onto the trail. Elevation 1,265 feet.

4.1 Cross the road again. Trail is signed straight ahead.

4.2 Go left (and uphill) on the Vista Trail. Elevation 1,430 feet.

4.5 Parking lot. Walk your bike through gate and continue uphill. Elevation 1,545 feet. The final section is very difficult.

4.8 The summit. Savor the views east toward the Seattle skyline and south toward Gold Mountain. The flashing lights in the near distance are at the Puget Sound Naval Shipyard. Elevation 1,665 feet.

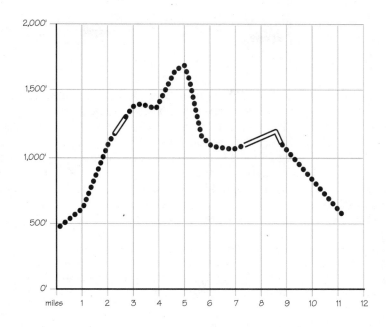

5.1 Reach the parking lot and proceed downhill on the Vista Trail.

5.3 Turn left on the Beaver Pond Trail. Elevation 1,400 feet.

5.7 Junction with Gold Creek Trail. Keep right on Beaver Pond. Elevation 1,275 feet.

6.9 Lots of trail hazards, including roots, concrete erosion-control blocks, rocks, and trail bumps, as you careen down to the Beaver Pond.

7.4 Cross road GM-1. Elevation 1,020 feet.

7.9 Climb some more. Elevation 1,065 feet.

8.3 The tread is better here but you'll still encounter the rogue rock or two. Elevation 1,130 feet.

8.4 Junction. Turn left on GM-3. Elevation 1,135 feet.

9.2 Just before you reach the campground, turn left on the Wildcat Trail. Elevation 1,110 feet.

9.6 Cross a gravel road. Elevation 890 feet.

9.9 Reach another road (most are not signed), go left and them immediately right on the trail. Elevation 775 feet.

11.3 Return to the trailhead.

Eastern Washington

It's been called the Cascade Curtain, and is used in the same sense as the invisible line dividing eastern and western sectors in post-war Europe, made famous by Churchill. There is no Checkpoint Charlie as you cross Snoqualmie Pass, but in many ways the Cascade Mountains are the dividing line between the largely urban Puget Sound and the farm and forest heartland of the east. The Cascades separate the two portions of the state into vastly different ecological and climatic territories. The west has a mild maritime climate that is wet and rarely hot for more than eight weeks or so per year; the east has extremes of heat in the summer months and snowy, freezing winters.

Warm weather comes earlier to the east side of the mountains, and that translates into drier riding when the trails on the west side are still soggy. Once you leave behind Seattle's burgeoning suburbs and cross into eastern Washington proper, you enter a whole realm of riding possibilities. There are entire watersheds with barely a dwelling in them.

Getting to trailheads east of the mountains can involve 30 miles or more of gravel road driving. But at other times, you can simply map out a ride by knitting together a route from a series of logging roads. That's what I did to create the Stampede Pass ride. Admittedly, it's not a singletrack but the next best thing—lightly traveled narrow roads. The solitude's just the same, even if the tread is a few feet wider.

The rides in this chapter cover a large area that I have called Eastern Washington. It excludes the two rides on the John Wayne Trail and the Spillway Loop ride. Since the first two form part of what will eventually be a cross-state trail, they are in the Puget Sound section of the book.

⌬ 37

Amabilis Mountaintop

Location:	6 miles northwest of Easton, in the Mount Baker-Snoqualmie National Forest.
Distance:	11.3-mile loop.
Tread:	Gravel and dirt roads.
Time:	2.5 to 3 hours.
Aerobic level:	Moderate.
Technical difficulty:	1–2.
Best time to ride:	April to October.
Facilities:	None.
Land status:	Wenatchee National Forest Ranger District.
Maps:	Wenatchee National Forest Ranger District.
Access:	From Seattle, drive east on Interstate 90 to Exit 63. Park at the Cabin Creek Sno-Park adjacent to the freeway.

Notes on the Trail

Amabilis is one of those brooding peaks that signals you're about to cross the Cascade Divide into western Washington (the "westside," as eastsiders put it). Many of the neighboring peaks are too steep for mountain bikers but, thanks to earlier logging activities, the ride up Amabilis is an easy undertaking up thoughtfully graded logging roads. And it's a sweet pleasure to descend. While you're up top it's worth the short detour to a rocky promontory where you can look north toward the Alpine Lake Wilderness. This makes for a quieter view than the west-bound, which includes the four-lane highway.

The Ride

0.0 From the Sno-Park, cross the interstate and head onto the gravel road. This is Forest Road 4826 signed to Kachess Lake. Elevation 2,470 feet.

0.3 Junction. Turn right on FR 4822.

1.3 The climb begins on a good, hard-packed dirt road. Elevation 2,850 feet.

2.3 Elevation 3,195 feet.

2.7 Junction with spur road 118. Keep left on the main road. Elevation 3,380 feet.

3.3 Heading north and up. Elevation 3,565 feet.

4.5 Pass a couple of unmarked tracks. Ignore these and keep heading uphill.

Amabilis Mountaintop

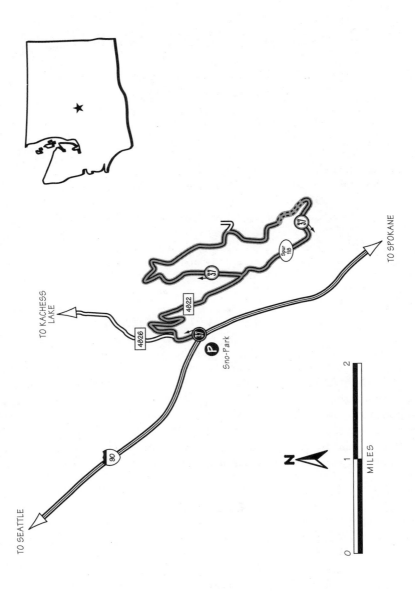

TO SPOKANE

TO KACHESS LAKE

37

Spur 118

37

4822

4826

37

P Sno-Park

90

TO SEATTLE

N

MILES

0   1   2

You can "bag" a craggy top on a short side trip at the top of Amabilis Mountaintop.

5.4 Pass unmarked road-end. Keep heading uphill. Elevation 4,360 feet.

5.5 Turn left on unmarked road. This takes you to the viewpoint. Park your bike and walk up the narrow path to the rocky area on your right. Breathe in the views from the top.

5.7 Turn left back onto FR 4822.

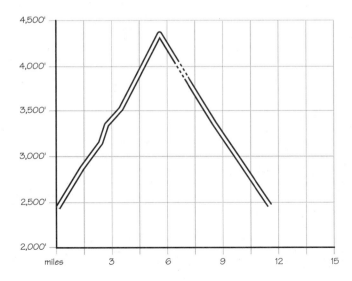

6.0 Road ends. On your right is a Cat track (as in *Caterpillar* tractor). Follow it into the woods.

6.3 Turn right on spur road 118. The downhill is about to begin. Elevation 4,385 feet.

8.4 You're now on the southern side of the mountain, overlooking the wide valley containing the interstate. Elevation 3,435 feet and dropping.

8.7 Rejoin FR 4822 and continue downhill.

11.0 Junction. Turn left onto FR 4826.

11.3 Return to vehicle at Sno-Park.

Coal Mines Trail

Location:	Cle Elum.
Distance:	6.6 miles, out and back.
Tread:	Loose gravel, former railroad.
Time:	1 to 1.5 hours.
Aerobic level:	Easy.
Technical difficulty:	2.
Best time to ride:	May to October.
Facilities:	Available in Cle Elum and Roslyn.
Land status:	Kittitas County; City of Cle Elum.
Maps:	USGS Cle Elum.
Access:	From Seattle, take Interstate 90 east to the first Cle Elum exit. Follow the exit road past Safeway and down the hill. Turn left on Stafford Avenue. You'll see a flagpole and an old mining car. Park between 1st and 2nd Streets.

NOTES ON THE TRAIL

Before Northern Exposure propelled Roslyn to fame as the fictitious Cicely, Alaska, it had a reputation as a tough mining village. The Northern Pacific Railroad fueled its steam engines with coal that was mined around Roslyn. This ride follows the old railway route used to haul the coal from the mines. As rail-trails go, it's on the short side and doesn't offer any spectacular bridges or tunnels. That said, Roslyn has several historical attractions, and the new trail is the best way to reach them. For now, the trail surface is rough and may be unsuitable for less strong riders.

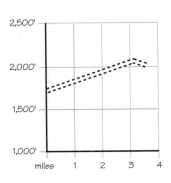

Coal Mines Trail

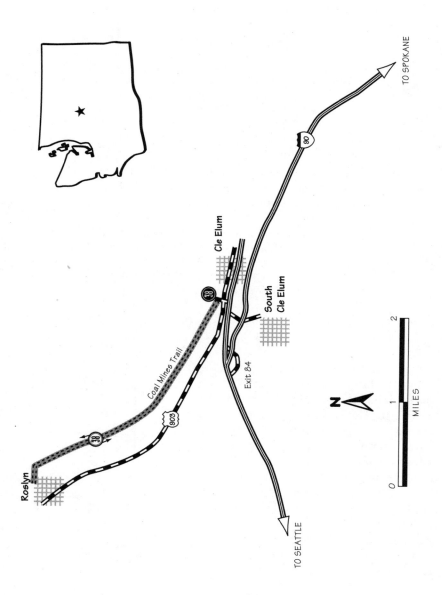

TO SPOKANE

90

Cle Elum

38

South
Cle Elum

Coal Mines Trail

Exit 84

903

38

Roslyn

TO SEATTLE

N

MILES

0   1   2

Roslyn, made famous as Cicely in TV's "Northern Exposure," looms at the end of the Coal Mines Trail.

THE RIDE

0.0 From the trailhead in Cle Elum, head out of town past the trail sign. Elevation 1,760 feet.

0.1 The trail starts off on rough stones, and with the indentations of the railroad ties. Elevation 1,780 feet.

1.6 Cross an access road. Keep straight. Elevation 1,940 feet.

2.5 The houses you see are on the edge of Roslyn. Here and there are remnants of the old mining days.

3.0 Cross another road, keep straight.

3.2 Cross another road, and just beyond, keep left where the trail forks. Turn left on North 1st Street. Elevation 2,105 feet.

3.3 Take the first right on Pennsylvania Avenue. You're now in downtown Roslyn. Retrace your route for the ride back on the trail.

39

Kachess Ridge Loop

Location:	9 miles northwest of Easton, in the Wenatchee National Forest.
Distance:	16.7-mile loop.
Tread:	Logging roads of packed dirt and gravel, some pavement.
Time:	3 to 3.5 hours.
Aerobic level:	Moderate.
Technical difficulty:	1–2.
Best time to ride:	April to October.
Facilities:	Flushing toilet and water at Kachess Lake Campground.
Land status:	Wenatchee National Forest, Cle Elum Ranger Station.
Maps:	Green Trails Kachess Lake; Wenatchee National Forest map.
Access:	From Seattle, take Interstate 90 eastbound to exit 62. Go left on Kachess Lake Road until you reach the campground at the end of the paved road. Park in the picnic area of the campground. Day fee or trailhead parking pass required.

NOTES ON THE TRAIL

There's nothing that beats a ride right from your tent. Bivie overnight at Kachess Lake Campground and pedal off in the morning for a moderate workout uphill and some satisfying downhill on well-maintained logging roads. As a bonus, you get a truly stunning view of the glacier-clad slopes of Mount Rainier. Go mid-week to avoid the inevitable power-boat set that fills the lakeside campground on summer weekends.

THE RIDE

0.0 Start at the campground gate and ride straight up the facing road. Elevation 2,215 feet.

0.4 There's a bulletin board at this intersection with FR 4948. Go left. The climb begins in earnest.

1.0 Some washboard below your tires as the road levels out briefly.

Kachess Ridge Loop

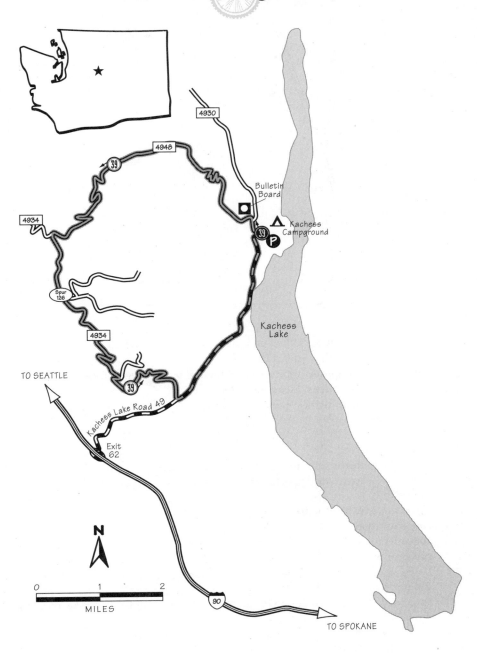

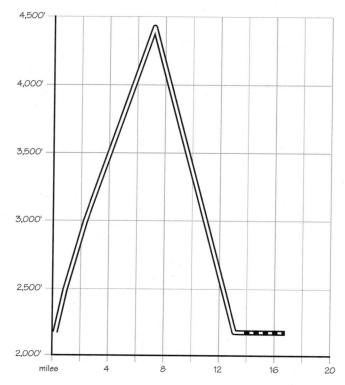

2.0 More climbing. Hit 2,885 feet and then 3,000 feet 0.2 mile later.

2.6 Short respite on a downhill section.

2.9 Views start to improve in this cleared section with younger trees.

3.0 Rough road with rocks. Elevation 3,250 feet.

4.0 You're on something of a plateau. Ahead, there's a notch between two hills. That's where you are headed.

4.2 Pass spur road 120.

4.4 Cross Gate Creek.

4.7 Unmarked intersection, follow the road to the right and uphill.

5.0 Pretend you are in Austria as the road climbs out of the clear-cut valley. Yodeling optional.

5.9 Cross the 4,000 feet mark.

6.4 Pass spur road 133.

7.0 Summit at 4,435 feet. It's downhill from here.

7.2 Junction with FR 4934. Go left.

7.4 If you're riding on a clear day, cast your gaze westward for an eyeful of Mount Rainier's snowy exterior.

8.5 Spur road 126 leads you uphill to more views. The road you're on keeps going down. It's your choice.

9.6 There's a sharp corner here at the start of a series of switchbacks on this mostly good surface.

13.2 Six miles of downhill are over so quickly. Go left on the pavement back to the campground.

16.7 A cooling lake and the comforts of your icebox await.

Lake & River Loop

Location:	9 miles northwest of Easton, in the Wenatchee National Forest.
Distance:	22.2-mile loop.
Tread:	Rough jeep road, gravel road, and some pavement.
Time:	4 to 5 hours.
Aerobic level:	Moderate.
Technical difficulty:	1–2.
Best time to ride:	April to October.
Facilities:	Flushing toilet and water at Kachess Lake Campground.
Land status:	Wenatchee National Forest.
Maps:	Green Trails Kachess Lake; Wenatchee National Forest map.
Access:	From Seattle, take Interstate 90 eastbound to exit 62. Go left on Kachess Lake Road until you reach the campground at the end of the paved road. Park in the picnic area of the campground. Day fee or trailhead parking pass required.

Notes on the Trail

A highly satisfying but undemanding loop on little-traveled forest roads. You get glimpses of a lake (Kachess) and a river (Yakima), plus the usual assortment of coniferous trees.

The Ride

0.0 Start from the Kachess Lake Campground and turn left on the paved road.

2.4 Left on Via Kachess Road. Ignore the sign that says "Dead End." It's not. You'll pass some two miles of fancy real estate that is the Kachess Community.

4.7 The pavement ends and Forest Road 4828 begins straight ahead, crowded by brush. This is a little used road unsuitable for most cars. Consequently, you're not likely to see any.

6.2 Pass spur road 124. You're riding through intimate woods and the lake is seldom visible through the dense foliage.

6.5 A stream flows across the road, making feet-wetting highly likely. Pick a crossing point carefully.

Lake & River Loop

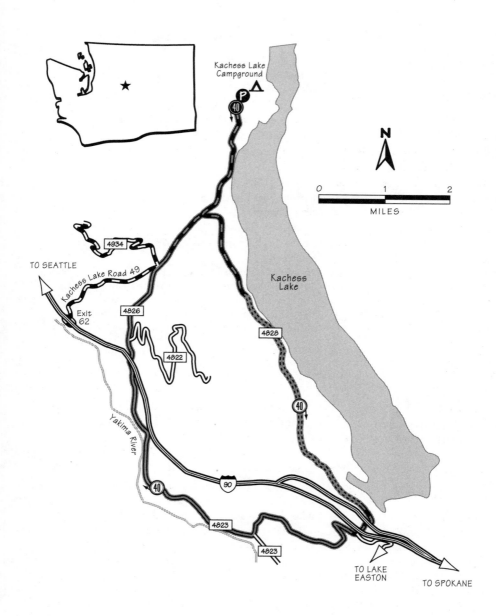

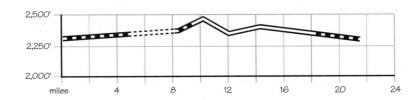

7.2 Daylight seems stark after the quiet darkness of the forest.

7.8 Delve back into the woods. You'll hear the rumble of I-90 in the distance.

8.1 Pass spur road 130.

8.8 End of FR 4828 and resumption of pavement (briefly). Take the first right and proceed under the freeway. The pavement ends again at a turnaround for trucks. Keep straight here and turn right at the T-junction. Proceed uphill on what was the old highway over the pass.

9.5 An unmarked road goes uphill on the left. Keep right and round the hill on your left.

10.5 Unmarked junction. Keep proceeding downhill toward the power lines.

12.5 Go under the high power lines. (And don't linger.)

12.7 At junction, go right on FR 4823.

13.0 The road parallels the Yakima River here. A good place to build a house, which some people have done in recent years.

14.9 Cabin Creek Sno-Park and U-fish pond is on your right. The store here sells chilled soda. The gravel road widens here and can be busy.

17.0 Cross over the freeway and proceed onto FR 4826. This gravel road is bumpy in places.

17.3 Junction with FR 4822. Keep left.

18.6 Rejoin Kachess Lake Road (FR 49). Go right.

19.8 Pass Via Kachess Road.

22.2 Return to campground.

41

Manastash Lake

Location:	20 miles west of Ellensburg, in the Wenatchee National Forest.
Distance:	7.6 miles, out and back.
Tread:	Singletrack.
Time:	2 to 2.5 hours.
Aerobic level:	Moderate.
Technical difficulty:	2–3.
Best time to ride:	June to October.
Facilities:	Vault toilet at lake.
Land status:	Wenatchee National Forest, Cle Elum Ranger District.
Maps:	Wenatchee National Forest.
Access:	From Interstate 90, take exit 109 toward downtown Ellensburg. In a half-mile, turn left on Umptanum Road. Follow it for 1.7 miles, and turn right onto Manastash Road. Proceed on Manastash for 10.8 miles until the pavement ends. This road becomes Forest Road 31, which you drive for 9.2 miles farther until the turnoff for Trail 1350 (Manastash Lake).

NOTES ON THE TRAIL

From the interstate it is hard to appreciate the geological forces that have shaped the wide valley that Ellensburg sits in. Once you get out of town on the backroads, you can delight in the rugged canyons that have been carved out of the basalt rock. There's also some backcountry that, while not wilderness, is still pretty wild. Manastash Lake is one of a handful of lakes that are very alluring during the hot summer months. Go midweek and enjoy a cool splash after a pleasing woodsy ride.

THE RIDE

0.0 At the trailhead parking lot proceed uphill behind the gate. Elevation 4,200 feet.
0.3 Where the trail crosses the road, turn right. Elevation 4,310 feet.
0.5 Leave a clear-cut area behind and enter the forest proper. Elevation 4,400 feet.
0.8 Cross a ridge and descend briefly into another valley.

Manastash Lake

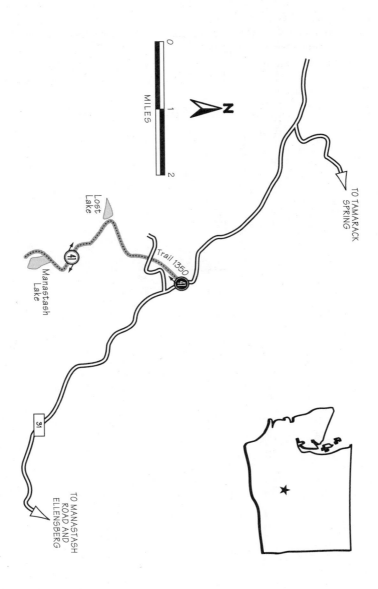

MILES

0
1
2

N

TO TAMARACK
SPRING

Lost
Lake

Trail 1350

4

4

Manastash
Lake

31

TO MANASTASH
ROAD AND
ELLENSBERG

★

1.7 Lost Lake. Elevation 4,715 feet.

2.2 Climb up through mature forest. Elevation 4,800 feet.

2.3 Badly eroded switchback. Elevation 4,845 feet.

2.6 Cross a creek. Elevation 4,920 feet.

3.1 Lots of fallen trees in this area. Steep climb starts. Elevation 4,975 feet.

3.5 First glimpse of lake.

3.8 Follow trail along the right shore of the lake. There's a pleasant area to sit and enjoy the lake before heading back.

7.6 Back at the parking lot.

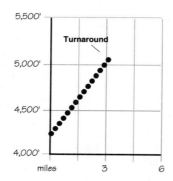

Manastash Loop

Location:	20 miles west of Ellensburg, in the Wenatchee National Forest.
Distance:	13.2-mile loop.
Tread:	Singletrack, jeep trails, some gravel roads.
Time:	4 to 5 hours.
Aerobic level:	Strenuous.
Technical difficulty:	4–5.
Best time to ride:	June to October.
Facilities:	Primitive toilet at lake.
Land status:	Wenatchee National Forest.
Maps:	Wenatchee National Forest.
Access:	From Interstate 90, take exit 109 toward downtown Ellensburg. In a half-mile, turn left on Umptanum Road. Follow it for 1.7 miles, turning right on Manastash Road. Proceed on Manastash for 10.8 miles until the pavement ends. This road becomes Forest Road 31, which you drive 9.2 miles farther until the turnoff for Trail 1350 (Manastash Lake).

NOTES ON THE TRAIL

This high-country ride combines trail, jeep road, and forest road to make a challenging half-day outing. There's more technical skill required on the descent than on the uphill, which has one extended section that's too steep for most riders to climb. The payoff is alpine scenery and a proving ground for your riding dexterity. Mount Rainier looms large to the west and provides stunning views. This ride completes a loop from the Manastash Lake ride but is considerably harder.

THE RIDE

0.0 At the trailhead parking lot proceed uphill behind the gate. Elevation 4,200 feet.

0.3 Where the trail crosses the road, turn right. Elevation 4,310 feet.

0.5 Leave a clear-cut area behind and enter the forest proper. Elevation 4,400 feet.

0.8 Cross a ridge and descend briefly into another valley.

Manastash Loop

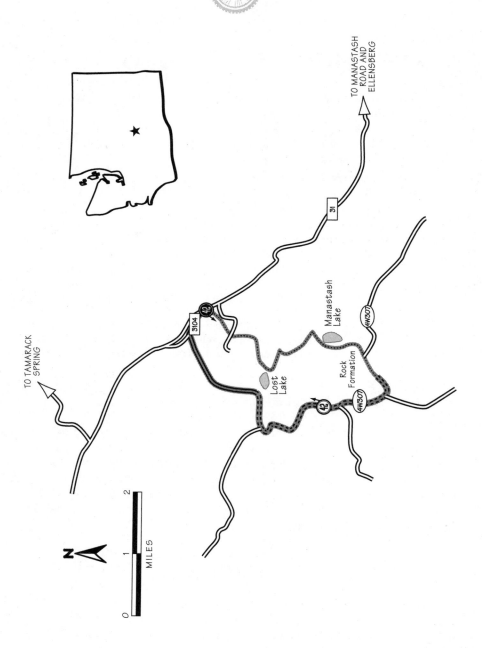

On the top of the Manastash Ridge.

1.7 Lost Lake. Elevation 4,715 feet.

2.2 Climb up through mature forest. Elevation 4,800 feet.

2.3 Badly eroded switchback. Elevation 4,845 feet.

2.6 Cross a creek. Elevation 4,920 feet.

3.1 Lots of fallen trees in this area. Steep climb starts. Elevation 4,975 feet.

3.5 First glimpse of lake.

3.8 Follow trail along the right shore of the lake until you see a trail rise steeply to the right. That's your trail. Elevation 4,940 feet.

4.3 After a strenuous and difficult climb (more of a push, really), reach the top of the ridge. Elevation 5,335 feet. Road 4W307 runs along the ridge and is signed in places and in other places is difficult to follow. This area is popular with owners of four-wheel-drive vehicles, and they don't always observe the rules of sticking to the assigned route. Keep the rock formation on your right and follow the worn route closest to the trees on your left.

5.0 Just after a treed area look for a triangle of roads. Take Road 4W307 as it continues right and uphill. Elevation 5,490 feet.

5.2 This is the highest point on the ride—5,640 feet. To the west is Mount Rainier's shiny mass. Get an eyeful of it as you begin the descent.

5.3 Junction. Turn right, staying on 4W307. Elevation 5,575 feet. You now start to double back on your earlier route to complete the loop.

5.8 Big lumps of basalt rock make it difficult to enjoy the view of Rainier as you pedal along a plateau. Watch for spur road 694 and turn right. This then magically becomes 4W307 again.

6.0 Keep right at two junctions after entering the woods. Look for a yellow sign that says "motor vehicle route." Elevation 5,570 feet.

7.0 Lots of roots and barrel-sized holes as you continue to descend. Elevation 5,535 feet.

7.3 Junction with 4W630. Keep right, staying on 4W307.

7.6 Cross a meadow. You'll see a building on the left among the trees. Keep right.

7.8 Ford a stream. Elevation 5,050 feet.

8.0 Junction with 4W308. Remain on 4W307.

9.0 The road levels out and is less bumpy. Elevation 4,855 feet

10.1 Traverse side of hill, climbing slightly in the process. You're now into an area that has been logged.

10.3 Road begins a descent into the valley.

10.7 Keep left at junction.

11.4 Descent to FR 3104. Elevation 4,250 feet.

12.1 Junction with FR 31. Turn right. Sign indicates 22 miles to Ellensburg.

12.9 Watch for Manastash Lake Lower Trailhead sign. Turn right onto singletrack here. Elevation 4,025 feet.

13.1 After you leave the wooded area, watch for the parking lot on the left. Turn left at the junction. Elevation 4,165 feet.

13.2 Return to vehicle.

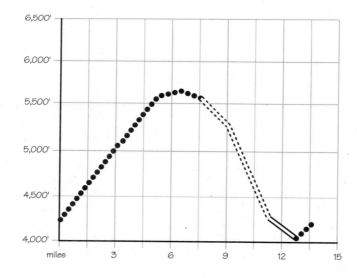

Spokane River Loop

Location:	Riverside State Park, 6 miles northwest of downtown Spokane.
Distance:	17.6-mile loop.
Tread:	Singletrack and pavement.
Time:	2.5 to 3 hours.
Aerobic level:	Moderate.
Technical difficulty:	1–2.
Best time to ride:	April to October.
Facilities:	Toilets and water at Riverside State Park.
Land status:	A joint project of Spokane Parks and Recreation, Spokane County Parks and Recreation, and Washington State Parks.
Maps:	Friends of the Centennial Trail map.
Access:	From Interstate 90 take the Maple Street exit in Spokane. Proceed north on Maple Street to Maxwell Street. Take a left on Maxwell and follow it as it heads down toward the Spokane River and becomes Pettet Drive and then, Downriver Drive, and finally the Aubrey L. White Parkway. Follow the signs to Riverside State Park.

Notes on the Trail

The parkway that leads to Riverside State Park commemorates visionary Aubrey L. White, who believed a city couldn't have too many parks. This ride provides a wonderful sampling of the attractive riverfront just a few miles away from Spokane's urban center. Although much of the route is on paved trail and roads, there's a surprising mixture of singletrack, quiet riverside

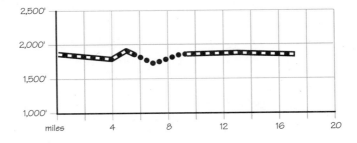

Spokane River Loop

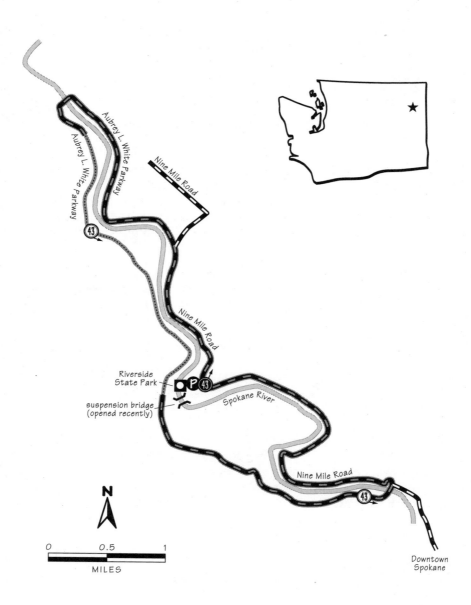

0 0.5 1

MILES

Downtown
Spokane

scenery, and bucolic woods to be found here. It's a good choice for family outings or beginners. A footbridge across the river to replace the one put up 50 years ago was completed in early 1999.

THE RIDE

0.0 Entrance to Riverside State Park. Turn left onto Aubrey L. White Parkway. Elevation 1,815 feet.

1.6 At Rifle Club Road, keep left on the parkway.

3.6 Ignore "Dead End" sign and continue to parallel the river.

4.2 Proceed around the blocks that prevent through traffic and turn left across the bridge. Elevation 1,690 feet.

4.4 After crossing the Spokane River, turn first left onto the Aubrey L. White Parkway. You'll see a Centennial Trail sign.

5.2 A gate bars the road here to vehicles. You'll see more trail signs. The main trail here is paved, but you should follow the dirt trail on the left that drops down to the river. Elevation 1,705 feet.

6.6 There's a smell of pine trees as you roll along beside the river. (This area may be very wet in the spring.)

7.4 Climb back up toward the paved trail and then drop back down. (Beginners may want to avoid the following section of the trail and stay on the pavement.)

7.8 The trail descends over rocks and is sandwiched between a rocky wall and the river. Elevation 1,680 feet.

7.9 Three-way junction: lower, middle and upper. Take the middle.

8.4 Trail meets up with lower trail. Keep right.

8.8 Four-way junction. Go straight across and uphill. You climb up 100 feet. (Or, turn left here to return to the Riverside State Park campground via the new footbridge, which is 0.2 mile beyond the junction.)

9.1 At the paved trail/road that crosses the park, turn left. Elevation 1,850 feet.

9.6 Park entrance. Enjoy the views from the thoughtfully provided benches overlooking the bluff. Then proceed down the paved road.

10.5 Turn left onto the signed trail. It's paved here.

12.2 Pass cemetery and follow trail signs. There's a restroom here.

13.4 Trail passes below and resurfaces next to the T.J. Meenach bridge. Cross the bridge. Elevation 1,795 feet.

13.7 Turn right and follow the trail to Pettet Drive. Turn right and cross under the Meenach bridge.

15.1 Turn left onto Downriver Drive, which becomes Aubrey L. White Parkway. You'll see signs for Riverside State Park. Elevation 1,775 feet.

17.6 Park entrance on the left. Elevation 1,795 feet.

Stampede Pass Loop

Location:	9 miles west of Easton, near Stampede Pass.
Distance:	18.3-mile loop.
Tread:	Dirt and gravel logging roads, some pavement.
Time:	4 to 5 hours.
Aerobic level:	Strenuous.
Technical difficulty:	2–3 (4 in one place).
Best time to ride:	May to October.
Facilities:	Vault toilet and water at Crystal Springs Campground.
Land status:	Wenatchee National Forest, Cle Elum Ranger District.
Maps:	Green Trails Snoqualmie Pass; Wenatchee National Forest map.
Access:	From Seattle, drive east on Interstate 90 to Exit 62. Go right for 1 mile to Crystal Springs Campground. Day fee or trailhead parking decal required.

NOTES ON THE TRAIL

Plum Creek, the timber company descended from the Northern Pacific Railroad, has been busy altering the landscape it inherited as railroad land grants. Great chunks of forest have been clearcut in the last two decades. The logging activity does leave a small consolation—a network of roads that won't see logging trucks for many years. This loop takes in a large section of little-traveled forest road that provides an inkling of what the railroad surveyors saw when they designed a tunnel to cut through Stampede Pass.

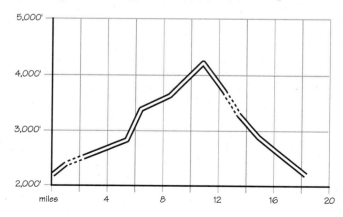

Stampede Pass Loop

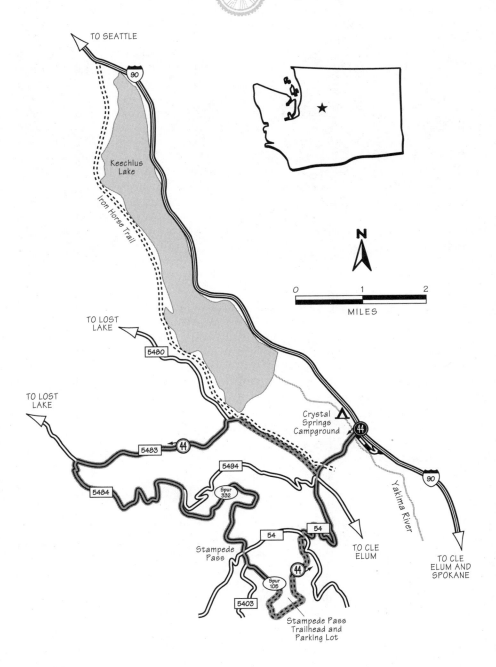

TO SEATTLE

90

Keechlus Lake

Iron Horse Trail

TO LOST LAKE

5480

TO LOST LAKE

5483   44

5484

5494

Spur 332

54   54

Stampede Pass

Spur 105   44

5403

Stampede Pass Trailhead and Parking Lot

Crystal Springs Campground   44

TO CLE ELUM

Yakima River

90

TO CLE ELUM AND SPOKANE

N

0   1   2
MILES

The corkscrew route back down from Stampede Pass.

THE RIDE

0.0   Start at the Crystal Springs Campground. Turn right on the paved road and cross the Yakima River.

0.7   Junction with Forest Road 5480. Keep straight.

0.9   Turn right onto the Iron Horse State Park Trail (the former Milwaukee Road rail line over Snoqualmie Pass: see also ride 4, Iron Horse State Park, on page 28). Elevation 2,275 feet.

2.5   When you reach the white gate, go left on FR 5480.

2.6   Go left on FR 5483, following signs for "Meadow Pass" and "PCT 2000." This is a good mainline logging road. Can be dusty in the summer.

3.0   The climbing is underway. You've reached 2,450 feet.

4.0   Still rising gently up a pretty river valley, sprinkled with old trees and newer firs.

4.3   Spur road 114. Keep straight.

5.6   Go left on FR 5484, a less maintained road most suited to high-clearance vehicles and mountain bikes. Elevation 2,840 feet.

6.1   Unmarked road to the left. Keep straight on FR 5484. Look for orange markers installed by snowmobilers.

6.5   Things are warming up. Elevation now 3,350 feet.

7.0   There's a waterfall amid a grove of trees that beckons as a rest area.

8.0   Unmarked spur, keep left.

8.5   An elevation of 3,695 feet provides good views over Keechelus Lake.

8.8   Junction with spur road 332. Keep right here: FR 5484 goes downhill, you stay on the uphill route.

9.3 Cross the 4,000-foot barrier and keep climbing.

9.7 You peak at 4,120 feet and begin descending. The pale scar on the far left is actually I-90 descending Snoqualmie Pass.

9.8 Keep right as you descend through a pleasant vale of firs.

10.2 There's a minor climb before the perfectly contoured 2.3-mile descent.

12.5 Junction with FR 54 and Stampede Pass. Go right and downhill.

12.7 Left on FR 5403. Elevation 3,440 feet.

13.0 Left on spur road 105. (It's shown on maps as FR 154.)

13.6 Cross the route of the Pacific Crest Trail.

13.7 Trailhead parking area, complete with toilet. Turn right on the road leading up to a lonely house.

14.2 The route is indistinct here. Follow the road under the electric lines and descend carefully on the sandy slope. When it levels out, follow the road to the left away from the pylons. Elevation 3,040 feet.

14.9 Junction with FR 41. Go left.

15.0 Junction with FR 54. Go right. Elevation 2,975 feet. If you're lucky there won't be any traffic on FR 54 as you breeze down it. But be prepared for cars, and the occasional logging truck.

17.4 Cross the route of Iron Horse State Park but stay on FR 54.

18.3 Return to campground.

Methow Valley

Mountain bikers never tire of raving about the Methow Valley. And for good reason. It seems made for bikes the way Scottish links were made for golf. What's more, the valley leaves the welcome mat out for two-wheelers.

The "Methow" lies between two wilderness areas—Lake Chelan/Sawtooth and the Pasayten—and encompasses a broad drainage basin that flows into the Methow River and, ultimately, south into the Columbia.

Hemmed in by mountains on three sides, the Methow has developed its own character as a result of its relative isolation (Washington Highway 20 from the west didn't open until 1972). Generous snowfall helped generate locals' penchant for cross-country skiing in the wide valley floor. This led to the creation of the Methow Valley Sport Trails Association, and the area's reputation as one of the best places in the country to strap on narrow skis. It was a natural extension to embrace mountain biking utilizing the ski trails in the spring, summer, and fall.

By combining existing forest roads with the ski trails, the Methow Valley quickly had a ready supply of riding places well ahead of most other areas of Washington. As mountain biking has grown, so too have the popularity of the Methow as a place to ride and the number of trails there to ride on.

The valley's pre-eminence for mountain biking is celebrated each year in early October during the Methow Valley Mountain Bike Festival, when hundreds turn up for fun rides, races, and social events. By then, temperatures in the valley have fallen from summertime highs in the 90s to a more temperate 70 to 75 degrees F. The ability to carry water on longer rides should be a consideration for July and August visitors. Sun protection is also very important.

Despite the recognition of the valley as a mountain biking mecca, its trails are never truly crowded (apart from the festival), and you can often find yourself on spectacular singletrack with just your own riding companion. Most hikers seem more attracted to nearby wilderness areas than to the trails frequented by mountain bikers. That said, the usual caveats about other trail users apply.

Okanogan National Forest requires payment of a fee for overnight stays anywhere in the forest, whether at a designated primitive campground or sleeping in your car. In 1998 this cost $3 a night or $10 for up to three consecutive nights. An annual pass allowing unlimited stays costs $25.

Buck Lake

Location:	8 miles northwest of Winthrop.
Distance:	12.5-mile loop.
Tread:	Singletrack, gravel and dirt roads, pavement.
Time:	2.5 to 3 hours.
Aerobic level:	Moderate.
Technical difficulty:	2.
Best time to ride:	May to October.
Facilities:	Vault toilet at campground.
Land status:	Okanogan National Forest, Twisp Ranger District.
Maps:	Okanogan National Forest, Twisp Ranger District west half.
Access:	From Winthrop, turn right on Chewuch Road opposite the Forest Service information office and ranger station at the west end of town on Washington 20. Proceed up Chewuch for 7 miles to a small campground (Memorial Campground) on the right. Park there.

NOTES ON THE TRAIL

The quintessential Methow riding experience is to breeze along interesting and varied singletrack, get an eyeful of views, take a few technical challenges, and have an overall good time. For good measure, a body of water always adds to the collection of memories. This loop has it all. If you are a confident navigator, you can extend the ride west toward Buck Mountain, where there are additional trails. Another option is to camp in the small campground next to Buck Lake and spend a day exploring and getting lost. The lake will beckon at the end of a hot day.

THE RIDE

0.0 From the Memorial Campground on West Chewuch Road, turn right on the paved road.

2.1 Turn left on Forest Road 5130, signed to Buck Lake. Elevation 1,930 feet.

2.6 After crossing a cattle guard, turn left on spur road 100. Elevation 2,120 feet. You'll see a sign for Buck Lake. This is the steepest part of the ride.

Buck Lake

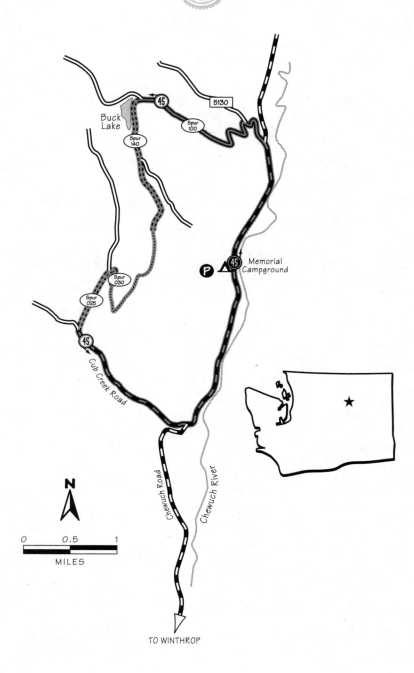

The combination of open chaparral-like countryside and forest make the Methow Valley an eye-pleasing ride venue.

4.9 When the lake comes into view, keep left toward the boat ramp on spur road 140. Elevation 3,200 feet.

5.3 After passing a gate, the road divides. Keep right.

5.8 Junction. Keep right. Road 140 begins to descend and deteriorates to an ever-narrower track.

7.1 Reach an open meadow with large shade trees. Keep straight. Don't go on the uphill trail. The road narrows here to two jeep tracks.

7.6 The jeep track becomes a singletrack as you traverse a hillside with views across the Chewuch Valley.

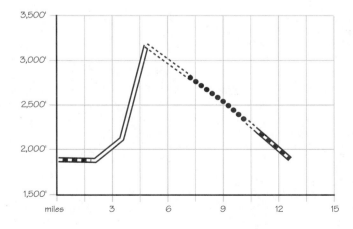

8.1 Enter a thin grove of trees as you continue crossing the hill.

8.4 Begin a descent as the track—often hidden by vegetation in the late summer—goes around the slope of the hill you just rounded. This meets up with another track at 90 degrees. Turn left and proceed downhill.

8.8 Junction of spur road 030 and spur road 025. Turn left and continue downhill. Elevation 2,695 feet.

9.6 Junction. Turn left on Cub Creek Road. Descend for almost 2 miles on the pavement.

10.5 Junction. Turn left on West Chewuch Road.

12.5 Return to vehicle at Memorial Campground.

Cooney Lake

Location:	About 18 miles southwest of Twisp, in the Okanogan National Forest.
Distance:	18.3 miles, out and back.
Tread:	Singletrack.
Time:	4 to 6 hours.
Aerobic level:	Strenuous.
Technical difficulty:	3–4.
Best time to ride:	June to September.
Facilities:	Primitive toilet at trailhead.
Land Status:	Okanogan National Forest, Twisp Ranger District.
Maps:	Okanogan National Forest, Twisp Ranger District.
Access:	From the town of Twisp, drive south on Washington Route 20 and WA 153 (toward Wenatchee) for 13.8 miles. Turn right on Gold Creek Loop Road for 1.5 miles. Turn right when you see a sign for Foggy Dew and Crater Creek Trailheads. Two miles later you'll pass the junction for Foggy Dew Campground. Keep straight and follow signs for Libby Creek. 1.5 miles after the pavement ends, turn left on spur road 300 and drive uphill for 3.5 miles until you reach Trailhead 431.

NOTES ON THE TRAIL

This is about as close as you can get to a genuine high-country wilderness experience on a mountain bike. Expect to meet backpackers returning from the Lake Chelan-Sawtooth Wilderness as you pound uphill toward Cooney Lake. The workout is worth the calories and sweat you will expend. The top consists of a huge natural bowl framed by the jagged Sawtooth Mountains. Set aside enough time to linger and partake of the wild and delicate beauty up here. Visit the lake on foot for the last quarter-mile to minimize erosion of the alpine flora. Then get ready for a challenging technical descent that requires constant concentration. Local riders make a loop out of this route by descending on the Foggy Dew Trail and then shuttling back uphill to the Cooney Lake Trailhead by car. Unless you have two vehicles, it's best to do this as an out-and-back ride.

Cooney Lake

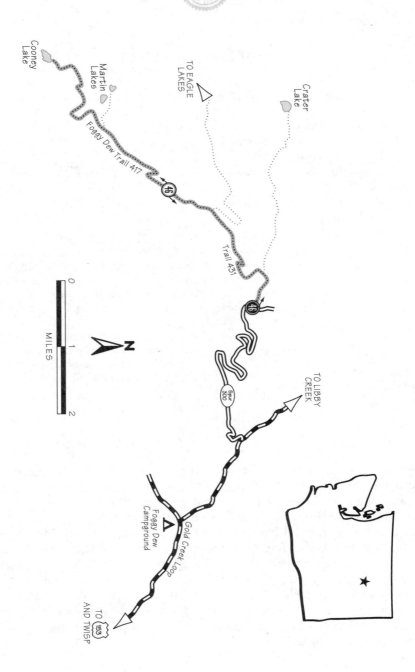

The ascent to Cooney Lake is gradual but persistent.

THE RIDE

0.0 Elevation 4,900 feet at the trailhead.

0.6 Tread starts off invitingly, but don't be fooled. Elevation 5,055 feet.

0.7 Junction with Crater Creek Trail. Keep left.

1.0 Elevation 5,095 feet.

1.5 Get glimpses of the forest below as you keep ascending. Elevation 5,340 feet.

2.0 Elevation 5,550 feet.

2.4 Junction. Keep left.

3.0 Descend briefly on smooth tread. Elevation 5,775 feet.

3.4 Walk your bike across this creek unless the water is really low. Elevation 5,455 feet.

4.0 You're back in the shade for the next section of uphill. Elevation 5,690 feet.

5.0 Elevation 5,890 feet.

6.0 Elevation 6,345 feet

6.8 Junction. Go left, following signs for Foggy Dew Trail 417. Elevation 6,645 feet.

7.5 Steep and rocky section. Elevation 6,820 feet.

8.0 Cross the 7,000-foot threshold. Elevation 7,030 feet.

8.5 Enter an alpine meadow with larch trees. Elevation 7,245 feet.

9.2 Park your bike here and follow the trail to Cooney Lake on foot.

9.2 The descent (with some uphill sections) begins.

11.1 Elevation 6,638 feet.

11.5 Junction for Martin Lake. Keep right.

12.8 Elevation 6,140 feet. Next section is rocky and bumpy.

14.0 Elevation 5,680 feet.

18.3 Trailhead.

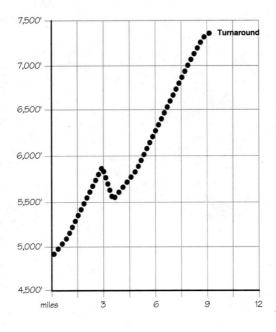

Goat Wall Loop

Location:	12 miles west of Winthrop.
Distance:	28.7-mile loop.
Tread:	Gravel, dirt, and paved roads.
Time:	5 to 6 hours.
Aerobic level:	Strenuous.
Technical difficulty:	2–3.
Best time to ride:	May to October.
Facilities:	Vault toilet at trailhead.
Land Status:	Okanogan National Forest, Twisp Ranger District.
Maps:	Okanogan National Forest, Twisp Ranger District west half.
Access:	From Winthrop, drive west on Washington Route 20 for 7 miles and turn right on Goat Creek Road (just before the bridge). Proceed 4.5 miles farther to the signed trailhead and Sno-Park on Forest Road 52. Turn right and continue up Forest Road 52 to the parking area.

Notes on the Trail

This loop packs a lot of punch in the calorie-consumption and scenic categories. It'll get your heart-pounding and your eyes widening. You climb up the massive hulk called Goat Wall, then descend into and climb out of the backcountry Black Pine Basin. Finally you descend back into the main valley on a rough jeep road. Purists may scoff at the notion of riding logging roads in the Methow when there is so much singletrack to choose from. Ride this loop and I think you'll agree it's a worthy contender for inclusion.

The Ride

0.0 From the trailhead parking area, turn right on FR 52. Elevation 2,090 feet.

0.7 Cross Goat Creek on a recently built bridge. The road moves inland as you climb.

1.9 Cattle guard. Elevation 2,545 feet.

2.4 Turn left onto FR 5225

3.0 Elevation 2,960 feet.

Goat Wall Loop

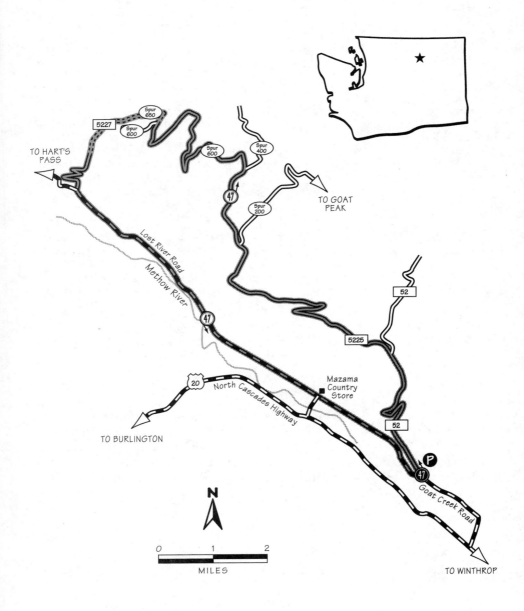

The plaque on the right records the names of mountain bikers who complete the Goat Wall Loop. (Just kidding.) It does name the surrounding peaks.

3.5   Road levels out briefly as you pass through a younger forest. Elevation 3,205 feet.

4.5   The vegetation is taking on a sub-alpine appearance. Elevation 3,515 feet.

5.6   Road switchbacks as it climbs to 3,860 feet.

6.4   Deserving views of the valley floor. Elevation 4,160 feet.

7.0   Viewpoint to admire the Methow up and down.

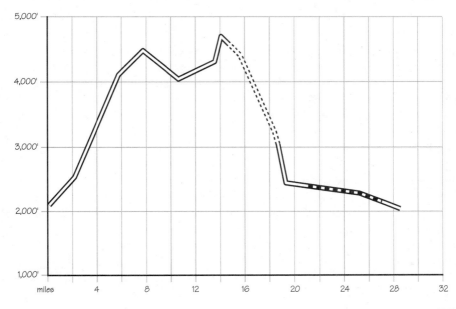

7.7 Road tops out here at 4,470 feet.

8.0 Cattle guard. Elevation 4,450 feet.

9.0 Junction with spur road 200. Turn right here for a stiff climb to Goat Peak. Or stay on FR 5225 for more fun.

11.0 After dropping into the Black Pine Basin, the road begins to climb again.

11.5 Elevation 4,150 feet.

13.0 Still climbing out of the valley. Elevation 4,320 feet.

14.3 Cattle guard. Elevation 4,735 feet. FR 5225 ends here and the road now continues as spur road 600.

15.8 As you round a corner, watch for spur road 650. It's easy to miss but does have an orange marker for a snowmobile route. Turn right. This short link takes you over to a rough jeep trail.

16.3 Turn left onto FR 5227, and prepare for a rough descent.

18.3 Elevation 3,295 feet. Last 1.5 miles of the road improves greatly.

20.6 Descend to the Yellow Jacket Sno-Park and trailhead. Cross the opening and turn left on the Lost River Road (paved). Elevation 2,435 feet.

26.8 Mazama Country Store has hot and cold drinks and snacks. Elevation 2,320 feet.

28.7 Turn left on FR 52. The parking lot is on the right.

Sun Mountain

Location:	9 miles south of Winthrop.
Distance:	6.6-mile loop.
Tread:	Singletrack.
Time:	1.5 to 2 hours.
Aerobic level:	Easy.
Technical difficulty:	1–2.
Best time to ride:	May to October.
Facilities:	Everything you want is available at Sun Mountain Lodge.
Land Status:	A mix of Forest Service land and private land.
Maps:	Sun Mountain Trails.
Access:	Heading south from Winthrop on Washington Route 20, turn right immediately after crossing the bridge at the edge of town. Unless you are staying at the lodge, park at the Chickadee Trailhead at the foot of the hill leading to the lodge. You can ride up the road to the start.

NOTES ON THE TRAIL

When the temperature begins to sizzle in the Methow—usually from June through August—a ride near Sun Mountain Lodge has obvious advantages. But the convenience of a full-service lodge at the end of the ride merely adds to the pleasures of pedaling in the area. All the trails are well signed and most are only a few miles long. Don't worry if you veer off the prescribed course, as there's an equally good ride to be found spontaneously. This ride is ideal for beginners or more experienced riders simply wishing to get in a quick pre-dinner mountain bike fix.

THE RIDE

0.0 With the lodge at your back and the volleyball court on your left, start off on the trail named Sunnyside. The trail descends through an open meadow. Elevation 2,900 feet. If you've parked at Chickadee, ride uphill to the lodge or follow a trail to the homestead.

1.6 After a gentle descent you enter an open area known as the Hough Homestead. An old house sits in the corner. Look for the trail exiting to the right of the house. Take the Lower Fox Trail. Elevation 2,710 feet.

Sun Mountain

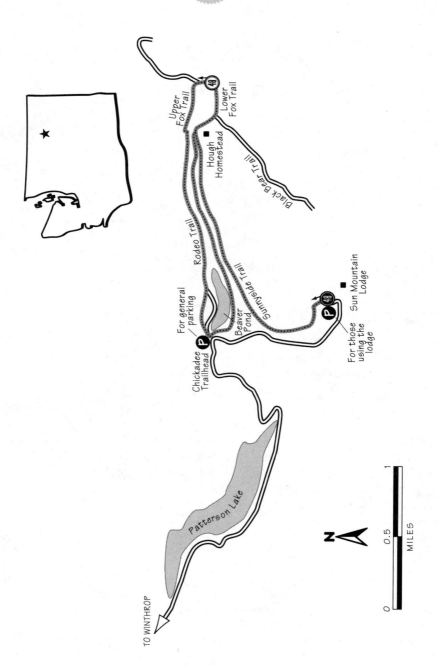

Upper Fox Trail
Lower Fox Trail
Hough Homestead
Black Bear Trail
Rodeo Trail
Sunnyside Trail
Beaver Pond
Sun Mountain Lodge
For general parking
For those using the lodge
Chickadee Trailhead
Patterson Lake
TO WINTHROP

MILES
0   0.5   1

All that countryside and a fine lodge at the top of the hill, too.

1.8 Junction with the Black Bear Trail. Keep left on the Lower Fox. Elevation 2,685 feet.

2.2 Junction with Upper Fox Trail. Turn left. Elevation 2,785 feet.

2.4 Crossroads. Go straight over onto Rodeo Trail. This parallels a stream as it drops down the valley floor. Elevation 2,725 feet.

3.5 Junction. Go left for Chickadee Trailhead.

3.6 Chickadee Trailhead. Go left onto Beaver Pond Trail. Elevation 2,680 feet.

3.9 Stay on Beaver Pond as it rounds the eponymous body of water. Elevation 2,750 feet.

5.0 Just as the Hough Homestead comes into view, watch for the Sunnyside Trail emerging on the right. Turn right and head uphill. Elevation 2,840 feet.

6.6 Reach the comfort zone of the Sun Mountain Lodge.

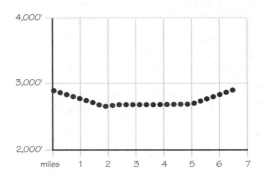

Thompson Ridge Loop

Location:	9 miles south of Winthrop, in the Okanogan National Forest.
Distance:	16.4-mile loop.
Tread:	Gravel and dirt roads, singletrack, some pavement.
Time:	4 to 4.5 hours.
Aerobic level:	Moderate.
Technical difficulty:	2–3.
Best time to ride:	May to October.
Facilities:	Primitive toilet at trailhead; Sun Mountain Lodge is nearby.
Land Status:	A mix of Forest Service land and private land.
Maps:	Sun Mountain Trails.
Access:	Heading south from Winthrop on Washington Route 20, turn right immediately after crossing the bridge at the edge of town. Follow the signs for Sun Mountain Lodge and park at the Chickadee Trailhead, 0.75 mile downhill from the lodge.

NOTES ON THE TRAIL

The Methow Valley Sport Trails Association has done a great job of creating a series of interesting trails to add to the ones already existing at Sun Mountain Lodge. What began as routes for cross-country skiers handily translated into spring, summer, and fall trails for mountain bikers of all abilities. This route, which knits together several short trails to create a loop, takes in some of the best singletrack in the area. There are lots of exciting downhill, technical areas, and a testing uphill section on one of the harder trails, Black Bear. Various points of the ride also provide expansive views of the Methow and the surrounding mountains. When you're done, a cool lemonade on the patio at the lodge is fully justified.

Thompson Ridge Loop

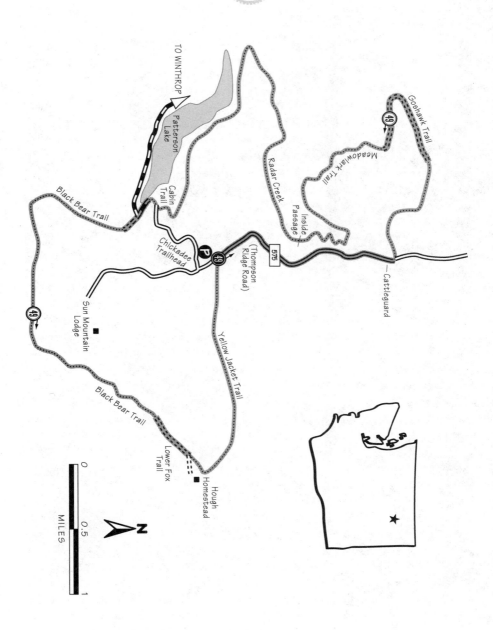

TO WINTHROP

Patterson Lake

Black Bear Trail

Cabin Trail

Chickadee Trailhead

(Thompson Ridge Road)

575

Radar Creek

Inside Passage

Meadowlark Trail

Goshawk Trail

Cattleguard

Sun Mountain Lodge

Yellow Jacket Trail

Black Bear Trail

Lower Fox Trail

Hough Homestead

0

0.5

1

MILES

N

Packs of riders are common on Sun Mountain Trails during the annual Mountain Bike Festival.

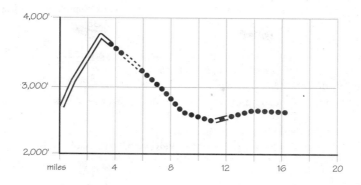

THE RIDE

0.0 From the Chickadee Trailhead, head uphill on FR 575. Elevation 2,600 feet.

1.2 This is a good gravel road with views over the valley as you climb. Elevation 3,110 feet.

2.2 Elevation 3,530 feet.

3.0 Elevation 3,700 feet

3.3 After crossing a cattle guard, look for a narrow trail on the left. Elevation 3,670 feet.

3.4 Look for mile marker 5 on the left and a sign for "Goshawk." Elevation 3,635 feet.

3.8 You swoop down a short section of singletrack that's steep but exhilarating. Turn left onto the Meadowlark Trail at the bottom. Elevation 3,375 feet.

4.4 Junction. Keep left on Meadowlark. Elevation 3,340 feet.

5.5 Traverse the side of the hill. Range cattle roam throughout this area. Elevation 3,380 feet.

6.0 Junction. Stay left on Meadowlark.

6.8 Smooth and potentially fast downhill. At the junction, keep right and follow signs for lower Inside Passage. Elevation 3,220 feet.

6.9 Junction. Go right on Inside Passage. A descent follows; rough in places.

7.5 Junction. Keep right (effectively straight ahead) and follow signs for Radar Creek. Elevation 2,925 feet.

7.7 Stock gate. Leave it as you find it.

8.5 Second stock gate. Lots of trail challenges here—rocks, roots, bumps, and bridges.

8.8 Elevation 2,620 feet.

9.1 Descend to an irrigated field. Go left for Patterson Lake. Elevation 2,570 feet.

10.6 A series of ups and downs as you ride along the side of the lake. Trail has drop-offs and is narrow in places.

10.7 Go right on Cabin Trail.

10.9 Cabin Trail ends at the Patterson Lake cabins. Cross the entrance road to the cabins and proceed straight and onto the Winthrop Trail. Elevation 2,575 feet.

11.1 Cross the Patterson Lake Road and go through the gate on the other side.

11.8 Junction. Keep straight for Black Bear Trail to complete the loop. (Or go right and proceed into Winthrop.)

12.7 Trail climbs for about a half-mile until reaching a short plateau, which provides fine panoramas of the North Cascades. Elevation 2,525 feet.

13.1 Steep downhill section with loose rocks and sandy soil.

14.0 In and out of small woods to an open hillside. Elevation 2,665 feet.

14.5 Back among big trees. Elevation 2,695 feet.

14.7 Turn left onto Fox Loop. Elevation 2,770 feet.

14.9 Cross Hough Homestead meadow to the bridge on the southside. Follow signs for Yellow Jacket Trail. Elevation 2,820 feet.

15.1 Turn left onto Yellow Jacket singletrack.

16.4 Cross the gravel road and follow the well-worn path back to the parking lot.

Northeast Washington

In the forested northeast corner of Washington, you can drive for hours before reaching a town of any size. Indeed, there are barely a half-dozen towns in the four counties that make up this huge swath of the state. Okanogan County, at 5,300 square miles, is bigger than several New England states combined. Add in Ferry, Stevens, and Pend Oreille and you have a huge chunk of real estate whose year-round residents would about fill a football stadium.

The northeast has plenty of public land—mostly National Forest land—but mountain bikers are relatively rare among the full-time residents of this part of rural Washington. Hopefully, land managers will soon recognize the economic benefits that mountain bikers can bring to rural forest communities.

Since the drive from western Washington to Colville National Forest takes the better part of a day (six to eight hours), the rides in this chapter will be best combined as part of a longer excursion for folks from the Puget Sound area. Spokane riders may also want to consider a weekend trip in this area, rather than crushing in a long day's drive on two-lane highways. If you do decide to spend a long weekend or a week in the northeast corner you'll find uncrowded trails and lots of roads that wind lazily through little-known mountain ranges.

Few trails have been developed specifically for mountain bikes, but many trails are multi-purpose. And be warned, trailheads are often far from paved roads in this region. Also, in some instances, completing a loop involves a long road ride at the end. Making such rides high on enjoyment and low on slog involves the use of two vehicles.

If you decide to venture out on your own, be aware that reaching certain trailheads is tricky, if not impossible, without a high-clearance, four-wheel-drive vehicle. The starts of the rides I have included can be reached by regular cars.

Recent winters have damaged roads and trails in the Colville National Forest, and a number of trails were either inaccessible or closed during my research in the summer of 1998. Check with the ranger stations to find out about current conditions before making plans.

Although northeast Washington is on the "dry" side of the Cascades and enjoys a long, hot summer, winters start early here and it often becomes too cold for tent camping much after the Labor Day holiday.

Frater Lake

Location:	29 miles east of Colville.
Distance:	4.3-mile loop.
Tread:	Singletrack, some dirt logging road.
Time:	45 minutes to 1 hour.
Aerobic level:	Easy.
Technical difficulty:	1–2.
Best time to ride:	May to October.
Facilities:	Vault toilet at trailhead.
Land Status:	Colville National Forest, Colville Ranger District.
Maps:	Colville National Forest.
Access:	From Colville, drive east on Washington Route 20 for approximately 20 miles to the Little Pend Oreille Lakes Recreation Area. You'll pass a series of lakes. About 29 miles out of Colville, look for the Frater Lake Trailhead on the left.

NOTES ON THE TRAIL

This ride is an appetizer to the wonderful selection of trails in the Pend Oreille Lakes area. Plus, it has all the right mixture of trail conditions to give a beginner a true flavor of singletrack riding. It's also well signed and you can even enjoy the comforts of the well-built warming hut maintained by volunteers. Part of the trail is open to motorcycles. Look for the blue diamond signs throughout the trail route.

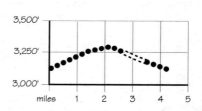

THE RIDE

0.0 From the trailhead follow the trail away from the parking lot. Elevation 3,115 feet.
0.2 Go left on the Coyote Rock Loop.
0.9 Ride through open forest. Elevation 3,175 feet.
1.5 Elevation 3,255 feet.
1.8 Keep right at ORV trail junction. Elevation 3,225 feet.

Frater Lake

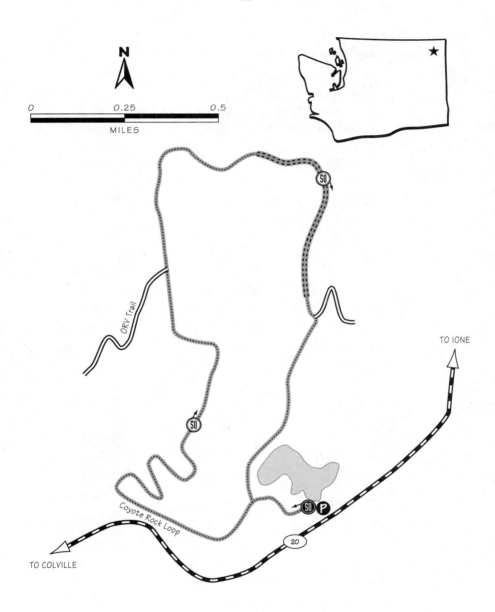

N

O — 0.25 — 0.5
MILES

ORV Trail

TO IONE

50

50

Coyote Rock Loop

50 P

20

TO COLVILLE

2.3 Elevation 3,288 feet.

2.4 Trail joins a dirt road. Logging took place in the summer of 1998. Follow the road downhill until you reach a junction with the trail on your right. The entire route is signed. Look for a blue diamond on a tree.

2.7 Turn right onto the trail and descend to a gravel road.

3.1 This section is boggy.

3.2 You'll see a deer fence straight ahead. Turn right, roughly paralleling that fence. Elevation 3,205 feet.

3.5 Cross over road to the trail.

4.0 After crossing a wooden cattle guard, enter the fenced area where the warming hut is located. It offers a cool interior on hot days.

4.3 From the hut, head straight and then take a left back to the parking lot.

Herran Creek Loop

Location:	15 miles northeast of Republic, in the Colville National Forest.
Distance:	20.3-mile loop.
Tread:	Dirt and gravel roads, pavement.
Time:	2.5 to 3.5 hours.
Aerobic level:	Moderate.
Technical difficulty:	1–2.
Best time to ride:	June to October.
Facilities:	Vault toilet at Old Stage Trailhead.
Land Status:	Colville National Forest, Republic Ranger District.
Maps:	Colville National Forest.
Access:	From Republic, drive east on Washington Route 20 and then north on WA 21. You'll see the entrance to Curlew Lake State Park; 2.2 miles north of it, turn right on Lambert Creek Road. This road is also shown on maps as Ferry County Road 546. Drive east on this gravel road, which becomes Forest Road 2165, for 5.5 miles until you reach Herran Creek Road. (When repairs are complete you can drive 2.5 miles farther until you reach the trailhead just beyond where the road was washed out when this ride was researched in 1998.) Park here.

NOTES ON THE TRAIL

An optimistic mountain biker may hope that if enough people visit this part of the Colville National Forest, more trails will surely follow. This ride is a case in point. It goes through a pleasing area that could be enhanced with a trail or two that would allow several loop options. Confession: This ride isn't perfect. It has no singletrack and includes a section of paved WA 21. But for sheer aerobic activity and peacefulness, it's a good choice. You get a gradual climb up through forested land, views, good compacted dirt tread and, thanks to a wash-out at the start, few vehicles. That, plus a downhill to satisfy the luge riders in us all.

Herran Creek Loop

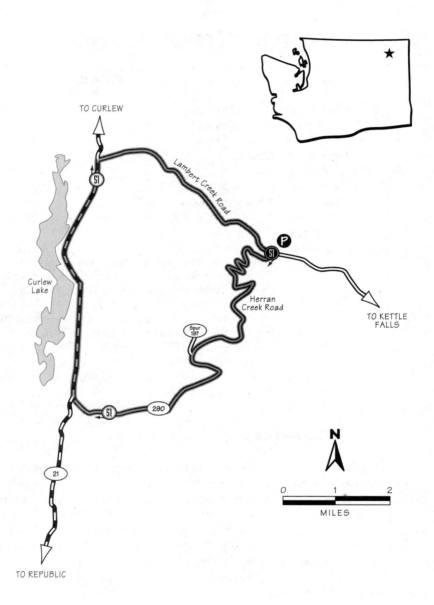

TO CURLEW

Lambert Creek Road

51

Curlew
Lake

Herran
Creek Road

Spur
197

P

51

TO KETTLE
FALLS

51 290

21

TO REPUBLIC

N

0 1 2

MILES

0.0   Head down Herran Creek Road (also signed as "Herrin" and "Herron" in various places). Elevation 3,885 feet.

0.1   Flooding has washed out the stream culvert. Pick a dry route across the creek.

1.0   Climb up on a well-compacted dirt road. You'll get glimpses east to Kettle Ridge. Elevation 4,010 feet.

2.0   Still climbing gently. Elevation 4,280 feet.

2.4   Cattle guard. Elevation 4,410 feet.

3.1   Still heading up at a reasonable elevation gain per mile. Elevation 4,525 feet.

3.5   First steep section. Elevation 4,600 feet.

4.0   Road levels out as you pass a high meadow. Elevation 4,640 feet.

4.9   If you don't want to do the whole loop, turn around when you see spur road 197. Elevation 4,685 feet. For loop riders, the road begins to descend.

6.3   Elevation 4,430 feet.

7.0   Exit Colville National Forest at cattle guard. Elevation 4,315 feet. You're now on Ferry County Road 290.

9.2   Smooth gravel road descends steadily past homes. Elevation 3,565 feet.

10.5 Junction. Turn right on WA 21. Elevation 3,205 feet. There's a shoulder on the highway here.

12.6 Pass the entrance to Curlew State Park. The pavement loses its shoulders for the next section. Elevation 3,235 feet.

15.8 Junction. Turn right on Lambert Creek Road/Ferry County Road 546. Elevation 3,195 feet.

18.1 Road initially has a reasonable grade and a good gravel surface. Elevation 3,475 feet.

19.1 Road begins to climb more. Elevation 3,630 feet.

20.0 Elevation 3,880 feet.

20.3 Turn right on Herran to return to your vehicle.

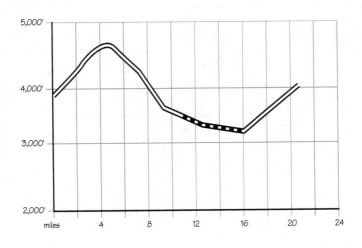

Sullivan Lake

Location:	5 miles east of Metaline Falls, in the Colville National Forest.
Distance:	29.2-mile loop.
Tread:	Gravel and dirt logging roads, some pavement.
Time:	6 to 7 hours.
Aerobic level:	Strenuous.
Technical difficulty:	2–3.
Best time to ride:	June to September.
Facilities:	Vault toilet and water at Sullivan Lake Campground.
Land Status:	Colville National Forest, Sullivan Lake Ranger District.
Maps:	Colville National Forest.
Access:	From Spokane drive north on U.S. Highway 2 to Newport and then continue toward the Canadian border on Washington Route 20 and WA 31 until just before Ione. Turn right (east) on Pend Oreille County Road 9345 until the north end of Sullivan Lake. If you're not camping, proceed past the ranger station to Forest Road 22 and park there.

NOTES ON THE TRAIL

This is Washington's wild corner, where there are millions of trees and lots of forest animals, but not too many people. This ride starts on FR 22, which runs 40 miles east, through the Selkirk Mountains separating Washington and Idaho, to Priest Lake. The ride climbs up toward Pass Creek Pass. It's a steady haul up the hill to the turnoff to a closed road that presents a near-singletrack experience, thanks in part to the regenerating vegetation. The road is gated for habitat restoration, which appears to be working. When the ride was researched in late summer 1998, two black bears were sighted. If you were so inclined, you could strap on panniers and make a three- or four-day trip on the backwoods roads that wander through the hills and valleys here.

Sullivan Lake

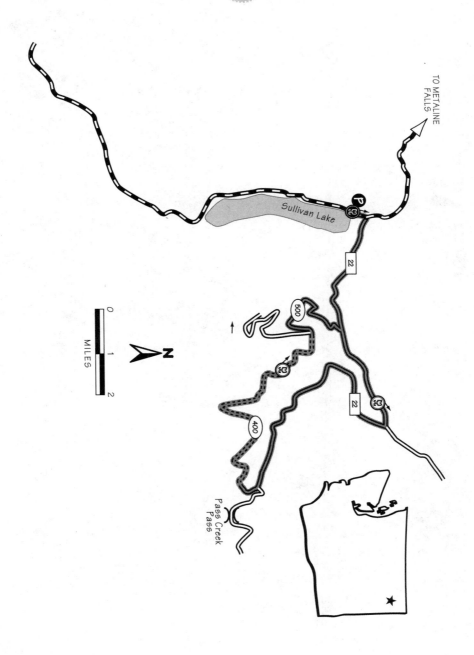

TO METALINE
FALLS

Sullivan Lake

22

500

400

Pass Creek
Pass

0
1
2
MILES

N

The end of this road offers the tantalizing Pass Creek Pass and ultimately, the state of Idaho.

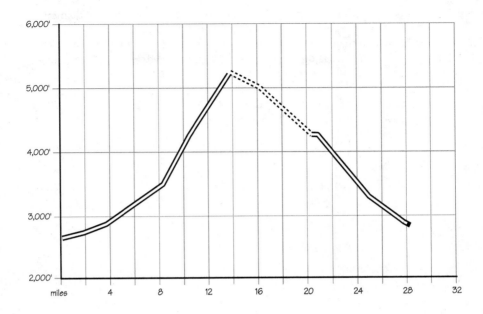

THE RIDE

0.0 From the Sullivan Lake Campground continue on the paved road heading north. Elevation 2,620 feet.

0.4 Turn right on FR 22

2.5 Good gravel road follows the scenic Sullivan Creek. Elevation 2,765 feet

3.7 Pass the junction with road 500. Elevation 2,860 feet.

6.0 Elevation 3,080 feet.

6.7 At a four-way intersection, stay on FR 22 as it turns right. Elevation 3,170 feet.

9.0 The forest is very shady here. Elevation 3,575 feet.

10.0 Gain views over the valley as you ride through a logged area. Elevation 3,945 feet.

11.0 Elevation 4,320 feet.

12.0 Elevation 4,605 feet.

13.0 Elevation 4,890 feet.

13.7 Junction with road 400. Turn right. Elevation 5,140 feet.

15.0 The road is partially grassed over and nicely rustic. Little maintenance takes place, so watch for obstacles and encroaching vegetation that may be wet in the mornings. Elevation 5,070 feet.

16.6 Elevation 5,020 feet.

17.5 The road descends gently down one side of the valley. Elevation 4,815 feet.

18.6 The road completes a horseshoe turn as it heads down the other side of the valley. Elevation 4,450 feet.

20.5 Small trees are filling the tracks of the old road. Prepare for several dismounts. Eyewear is a good idea to protect against wayward branches.

21.4 More scrub and then a slight climb through a forested area. Elevation 4,195 feet.

22.0 End of road 400. Turn right onto road 500 and head downhill. This road has loose gravel and is bumpy in places. Elevation 4,220 feet.

24.2 Elevation 3,445 feet.

25.4 Cross a bridge just before reaching FR 22. Elevation 3,005 feet. Turn left.

28.8 Reach paved road. Go left for the campground.

29.2 Sullivan Lake.

Old Stage

Location:	18 miles northeast of Republic, in the Colville National Forest.
Distance:	9.8 miles, out and back.
Tread:	Dirt and gravel roads.
Time:	2 to 3 hours.
Aerobic level:	Moderate.
Technical difficulty:	1.
Best time to ride:	June to October.
Facilities:	Vault toilet at trailhead.
Land Status:	Colville National Forest, Republic Ranger District.
Maps:	Colville National Forest.
Access:	From Republic, drive east on Washington Route 20 and then north on WA 21. You'll see the entrance to Curlew Lake State Park; 2.2 miles north of it, turn right on Lambert Creek Road, also shown on maps as Ferry County Road 546. Drive east on this gravel road, which becomes Forest Road 2165, for 5.5 miles until you reach Herran Creek Road. (If the road has been repaired, drive 2.5 miles farther until you reach the trailhead just beyond where the road was washed out when this ride was researched in 1998.) Park at Herran Creek, or if the road has been reopened, at the trailhead. Note: Old Stage Trail is due to re-open summer, 1999.

NOTES ON THE TRAIL

Heavy rains and flash flooding have wreaked havoc on trails and roads in this area. The forest has a backlog of repairs that may take years to complete. This has closed some very inviting riding areas (including Old Stage Trail 1) but created some new opportunities to travel on roads no longer accessible to motor vehicles. This is a good warm-up ride that provides a chance to see some of the storm damage up close and enjoy the solitude of a mountain road that's currently off-limits to cars. Check with the ranger station in Republic on the status of this area, as conditions will change as repairs are completed.

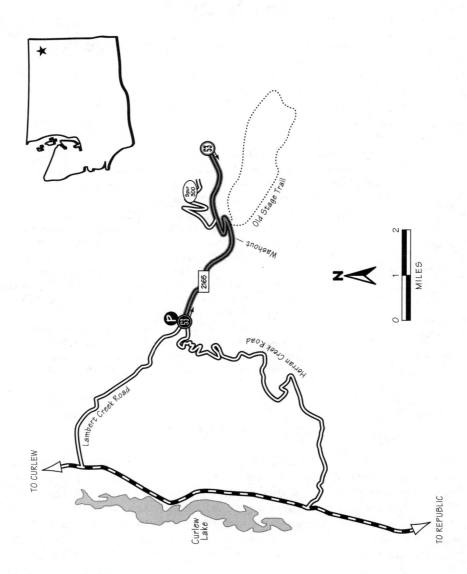

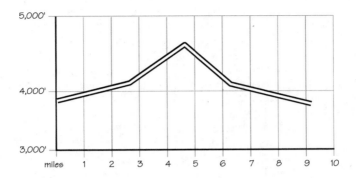

THE RIDE

0.0 Head uphill on FR 2165, passing some houses and ranches. Elevation 3,885 feet.

2.5 Reach the section of washed-out road. Scramble down the gash created by Lambert Creek. There's a worn route that will get you and your bike safely to the other side of the road. Follow it.

2.7 Reach the trailhead for the currently closed Old Stage Trail 1. A quick survey of fallen logs shows the impossibility of riding this trail. Not to worry. Keep left and proceed uphill on FR 2165. Elevation 4,150 feet.

3.6 Junction with spur road 300. Stay on the main route. Elevation 4,170 feet.

4.5 Continue climbing through open rangeland with views over the forested valley below. In the distance you'll see the Kettle Range and the burn zone from a major fire.

4.6 Reach a meadow. There are remnants of a logging operation and a few tracks that peter off in the woods. Turn around here and head back down. Elevation 4,595 feet.

6.9 Old Stage Trailhead. Elevation 4,150 feet.

7.3 Washed-out area.

9.2 Herran Creek Road and your vehicle.

54

Rattlesnake Loop

Location:	15 miles southwest of Republic, in the Colville National Forest.
Distance:	19.9-mile loop.
Tread:	Gravel and dirt roads, some pavement.
Time:	4 to 5 hours.
Aerobic level:	Moderate.
Technical difficulty:	1.
Best time to ride:	June to October.
Facilities:	Vault toilet and water at campground.
Land Status:	Colville National Forest, Republic Ranger District.
Maps:	Colville National Forest.
Access:	From Republic, head south on Washington Route 21 for 6.7 miles. Turn right on Scatter Creek Road (Forest Road 53), following signs for Swan Lake. After 7.5 miles, park at the day-use area at the Swan Lake Campground.

NOTES ON THE TRAIL

Forest managers have responded to mountain bikers by centering a series of bike trails in the scenic lakes area just south of Republic. Several routes use trails originally developed for motorcycles; others employ abandoned logging roads. Each year in late September, a mountain-bike festival takes place here. A variety of riding options makes it an ideal destination for a weekend or longer. This route uses logging roads that see little traffic as they wind through the forested backcountry. There's enough mixture of mature and younger forest to please the eyes and provide views. You can complete it as laid out here or combine it with the Swan Lake Loop (Ride 55) for a larger figure-eight ride that adds in a healthy dose of singletrack.

THE RIDE

0.0 From the parking area at the Swan Lake Campground, head back in the direction you drove in. Elevation 4,485 feet.

0.4 Pass the end of short loop around Swan Lake.

0.6 Junction. Turn right onto FR 5314, signed with a blue bike. Elevation 4,405 feet.

Rattlesnake Loop

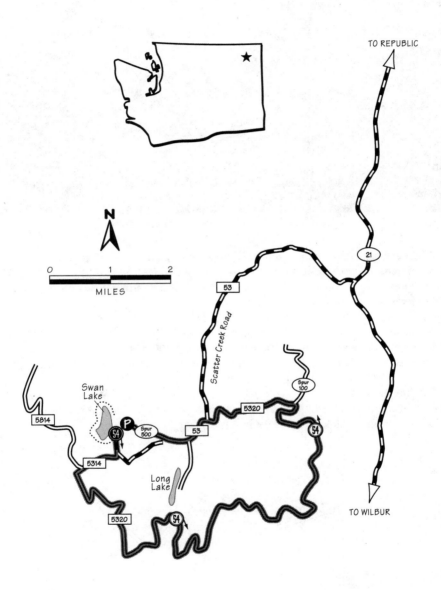

TO REPUBLIC

N

0   1   2
MILES

TO WILBUR

Scatter Creek Road

Swan Lake

Long Lake

21

53

53

5320

5320

5314

5814

Spur 100

Spur 500

P

54

54

54

54

Trees and solitude await riders wishing to tackle the Rattlesnake Loop.

1.0 Begin the first of many climbs. Cross a cattle guard at 4,460 feet.

1.3 Junction. Turn left on FR 5320. Elevation 4,170 feet.

3.2 The smooth road meanders down a valley following the contours of the topography. Elevation 4,170 feet.

4.4 Elevation 4,220 feet.

5.3 Road begins to descend again. Elevation 4,260 feet.

6.4 Now climb out of another valley. Elevation 4,100 feet.

7.0 Elevation 4,250 feet. The road continues to climb gently with long switchbacks that cling to the valley sides.

8.0 Elevation 4,455 feet.

9.0 Elevation 4,655 feet. You'll reach the highest point on the ride at 4,680 feet.

10.0 Elevation 4,645 feet. Let the descent begin.

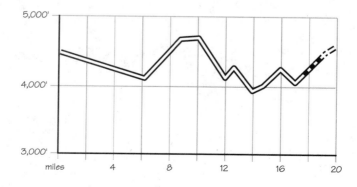

11.9 Downhills also pass at double-time. You're now at 4,155 feet, and begin to ascend again. Take a moment to take in the conifer-coating of the valleys and the brown, grassy hills to the east.

12.2 What goes up quickly comes down on this ride. Elevation 4,230 feet.

13.7 Elevation 3,935 feet.

15.0 Inevitably, the sign of the regulation-sized plantation conifers. Elevation 4,005 feet.

15.4 Stay left as you round this corner with spur road 100 on the right.

16.2 Elevation 4,205 feet.

17.2 Junction. Turn left on FR 53. Elevation 4,010 feet.

18.1 Turn right on spur road 500. Elevation 4,170 feet.

19.5 Junction. Turn right, back onto paved FR 53. Elevation 4,475 feet.

19.9 Reach trailhead.

Swan Lake

Location:	15 miles southwest of Republic, in the Colville National Forest.
Distance:	6.7-mile loop.
Tread:	Singletrack, gravel and dirt roads, some pavement.
Time:	1.5 to 2 hours.
Aerobic level:	Moderate.
Technical difficulty:	2–3.
Best time to ride:	June to October.
Facilities:	Vault toilet and water at campground.
Land Status:	Colville National Forest, Republic Ranger District.
Maps:	Colville National Forest.
Access:	From Republic, head south on Washington Route 21 for 6.7 miles. Turn right on Scatter Creek Road (Forest Road 53), following signs for Swan Lake. In 7.5 miles, park at the day-use area at the Swan Lake Campground.

NOTES ON THE TRAIL

You'll feel like doing pirouettes after circling this loop. It has as many twists and turns as an act from a ballet production, and you get to be the star. Among this ride's attractions are singletrack, no serious climbs, varied scenery, some technical downhill, some gravel roads, and even a short section of pavement. In other words, it has a complete repertoire of conditions that you'd want for a matinee ride. The route is even clearly marked.

THE RIDE

0.0 From the day-use parking area, head past the gate following the bike signs for road 075, an abandoned logging road. Elevation 4,530 feet.

0.1 Keep right at fork in the trail. Ride past the stock fence just beyond the fork. This is pleasant mature forest.

1.0 Elevation 4,480 feet.

1.1 Cross road and jog left onto the trail. Follow the bike sign.

1.4 Creek crossing. Elevation 4,325 feet.

1.5 Junction. Keep right; don't cross the cattle guard. Elevation 4,330 feet.

Swan Lake

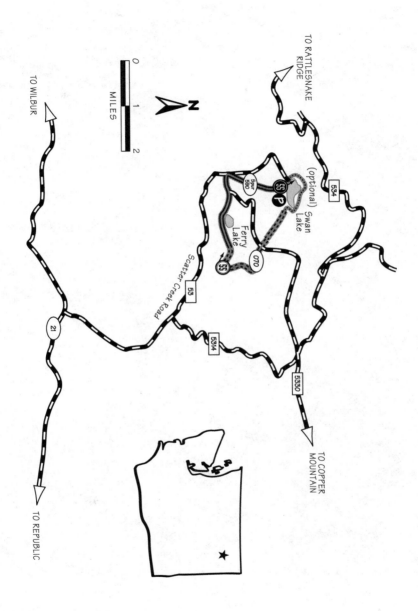

Great views from the trail around Swan Lake.

1.9 Cross another creek and over to a rough jeep track. Elevation 4,175 feet.

2.0 Junction. Go left. Elevation 4,165 feet.

2.1 Junction. Go right.

2.5 After crossing a cattle guard, take an immediate right and head downhill. You'll see Ferry Lake, and then ride down the side of it. Elevation 4,235 feet.

3.1 Follow the lake trail as far as it goes and then turn left on a gravel road leading uphill. Elevation 4,285 feet.

4.1 Junction. Turn right on FR 5330. Elevation 4,200 feet.

4.4 After cattle guard, turn right on FR 53.

4.6 Turn right on spur road 500. It's a quiet and unpaved alternative to FR 53. Elevation 4,205 feet.

6.0 Junction. Turn right on FR 53. Elevation 4,470 feet.

6.1 Turn left on spur road 070, following signs for the boat ramp.

6.5 Just before the lake, turn right on a trail snaking through the campground. Follow it to site T-4 and take a small road leading from the campground back up to the parking area.

6.7 Trailhead.

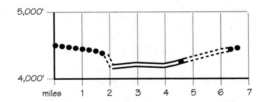

SWAN LAKE TRAIL OPTION

For hors d'oeuvre, try the actual loop around the west side of Swan Lake. You can add it to any of the rides in this area. It's technically challenging in places, with rocks, roots, uneven surfaces, wooden trestles, and more. You start from the trailhead at the day-use parking area.

Tread:	Singletrack.
Time:	30 to 45 minutes.
Aerobic level:	Moderate.
Technical difficulty:	2–3.

THE RIDE

0.0 With the gate leading to spur road 075 at your back, turn right at the small opening in the rail fence. Head down toward the lake. Elevation 4,425 feet.

0.1 Ride through an open, grassy area next to the lake before passing a group shelter. Beyond the shelter, the trail is easy to follow.

0.7 Wonderful woodland singletrack. Some ruts and roots. Elevation 4,395 feet.

0.9 Log bridge and then log trestle in poor condition.

1.2 Short, steep hill. Elevation 4,390 feet. This is probably the hardest section of the trail.

1.5 After crossing another trestle, awkwardly placed at 90 degrees to the tread, the trail smoothes out.

1.7 Trail's end at FR 53

2.2 Back to the parking area via the campground paved road.

Appendix: Resources

Puget Sound

Anacortes Community Forest Lands
P.O. Box 547
Anacortes, Washington 98221
(360) 293-1918

DNR South Puget Sound Region
28329 Southeast 448th Street
P.O. Box 68
Enumclaw, Washington 98022-0068
(360) 825-1631 or (800) 527-3305

King County RoadShare Program
(206) 689-4741

Mount Baker-Snoqualmie National Forest
White River Ranger District
857 Roosevelt Avenue East
Enumclaw, Washington 98022
(360) 825-6585

Pack Experimental Forest
University of Washington
9010 453rd Street East
Eatonville, Washington 98328
(360) 832-6534

Washington State Parks & Recreation
Commission
(800) 233-0321

Wenatchee National Forest
Cle Elum Ranger District
West 2nd
Cle Elum, Washington 98922
(509) 674-4411

South Cascades
Gifford Pinchot National Forest
Cowlitz Valley Ranger District
10024 Highway 12
Randle, Washington 98377
(360) 497-1100

Gifford Pinchot National Forest
Mount Adams Ranger District
2455 Highway 141
Trout Lake, Washington 98650
(360) 395-3400

Gifford Pinchot National Forest
Wind River Ranger Station
1262 Hemlock Road
Carson, Washington 98610
(509) 427-5645

North Cascades
DNR Northwest Region
919 North Township Street
Sedro-Woolley, Washington 98284
(360) 856-3500 or (800) 527-3305

Wenatchee National Forest
Leavenworth Ranger District
600 Sherbourne
Leavenworth, Washington 98826
(509) 548-6977

Kitsap and Olympic
DNR Olympic Region
411 Tillicum Land
Forks, Washington 98331
(360) 374-6131 or (800) 527-3305

DNR South Puget Sound Region
P.O. Box 68
28329 Southeast 448th Street
Enumclaw, Washington 98022-0068
(360) 825-1631 or (800) 527-3305

Olympic National Forest
Forks Visitor Center
551 Forks Avenue South
Forks, Washington 98331
(360) 375-7655

Olympic National Forest
Hood Canal Ranger Station
P.O. Box 68
Hoodsport, Washington 98548
(360) 877-5254

Olympic National Forest
Quilcene Ranger District
P.O. Box 280
Quilcene, Washington 98376
(360) 765-3368

Olympic National Forest
Lake Quinault Ranger Station
P.O. Box 43
Quinault, Washington 98575
(360) 288-2525

Eastern Washington
Friends of the Centennial Trail
P.O. Box 351
Spokane, Washington 99210-0351
(509) 624-7188

Mount Baker-Snoqualmie National Forest
North Bend Ranger Station
42404 Southeast North Bend Way
North Bend, Washington 98045
(360) 888-1421

Wenatchee National Forest
Cle Elum Ranger District
West 2nd
Cle Elum, Washington 98922
(509) 674-4411

Methow Valley
Methow Valley Sport Trails Association
P.O. Box 147
Winthrop, Washington 98862
(509) 996-3287

Okanogan National Forest
Twisp Ranger District
Twisp, Washington 98856
(509) 997-2131

Okanogan National Forest
Winthrop Ranger District West
Winthrop, Washington 98862
(509) 997-2131

Sun Mountain Lodge
P.O. Box 1000
Winthrop, Washington 98862
(800) 572-0493

NorthEast Washington
Colville National Forest
Colville Ranger District
755 South Main Street
Colville, Washington 99114
(509) 684-4557

Colville National Forest
Republic Ranger District
180 North Jefferson
Republic, Washington 99166
(509) 775-3305

Colville National Forest
Sullivan Lake Ranger District
Metaline Falls, Washington 99153
(509) 446-2681

Useful World Wide Web sites

The following Web sites might be helpful if you're planning on making a trip. You'll find some more useful than others but several have a good selection of links to other sites.

State and federal land

Washington State Department of Natural Resources
http://www.wa.gov/dnr/

Olympic National Forest
http://www.fs.fed.us/r6/Olympic/

Gifford Pinchot National Forest
http://www.fs.fed.us/gpnf/

Wenatchee National Forest
http://www.fs.fed.us/r6/wenatchee/

Mt. Baker-Snoqualmie National Forest
http://www.fs.fed.us/r6/mbs/

Mountain bike groups

Backcountry Bicycle Trails Club
http://www.bbtc.org

Single Track Mind Cycling Club
http://members.aol.com/STMClub/stmclub.html

International Mountain Biking Association
http://www.imba.com/

Others

Methow Valley Sport Trails Association
http://www.methow.com/ ~ mvsta/

Glossary

Our language is already cluttered with jargon and special terms. Land managers and mountain bikers have a few of their own. I have tried to keep the use of these words to a minimum. Here's a short list of some you may see in the book or hear on the trail.

ATB: All Terrain Bike. Favored use is now mountain bike.
Clean: As in complete a difficult section of trail without putting your foot down.
Catch air: When both wheels leave the trail simultaneously.
Clear-cut: Logging activity that razes all trees in a given area.
Crash & burn: Sometimes happens after you catch air.
Dab: Against your best wishes, when you put your foot down to prevent a heavy bout of gravity.
Endo: Head over handlebars.
Equestrians: People who ride horses.
Hairpin: A tight corner when a trail turns back on itself. Also known as a switchback.
Hardpack: A dirt trail of firmly compacted material. Good riding surface.
IMBA: International Mountain Bike Association; advocacy group for mountain bikers.
Jeep road: A rough road suitable for use only by vehicles with four-wheel drive.
Loop: A trail route that starts and finishes at the same point, usually without having to cover the same area twice.
Mainline: Principle logging road.
Multiple use: Trails open to numerous types of recreation. Always includes hikers and may include equestrians, mountain bikes, motorcycles, and even four-wheel vehicles.
ORV: Off-Road Recreation Vehicle; Washington State has designated ORV areas.
Old-growth: Trees that have grown naturally and may be hundreds of years old.
Out-and-back: When a ride is not a loop.
PCT: Pacific Crest Trail. Long-distance path that is closed to mountain bikes.
Pumice: Light, cinder-like volcanic rock that turns up on trails in the Gifford Pinchot National Forest, Mount St. Helens, and other places. Makes a crunchy sound when you ride over it.
Ruts: Deeply eroded areas frequently caused by motorcycle over-use.
Sidehill: When trail runs parallel to the slope of a hill and crosses it.
Singletrack: A trail no wider than a few feet that cannot be used by four-wheel vehicles. The most interesting mountain biking trail.
Snag: Trees that have fallen and are caught up in trees nearby.
Switchback: *See* hairpin.
Technical: Terrain that represents a challenge to ride over because of obstacles or changes in surface.

Topo: Short for topographical map that shows lots of detail.

Tread: The riding surface. It can be anything from a paved road to a root-infested singletrack.

Washboard: Vehicle suspensions cause these evenly spaced ridges on unpaved roads; makes for unpleasant riding or driving.

Wilderness: Land set aside under federal protection and closed to all mechanical intrusion, including bikes.

Whoop-de-doo: Trail undulations that mimic a roller coaster. Lots of fun.

Index

Page numbers in *italic* type refer to photographs.
Page numbers in **bold** type refer to maps.

About the Author

Gordon Black is a writer and public-radio producer who took to off-road cycling a decade before the invention of the mountain bike. He lives on Bainbridge Island, Washington.

Plan Your Next Outdoor Adventure at Our Website.

Since 1979, Falcon has brought you the best in outdoor recreational guidebooks. Now you can access that same reliable and accurate information online.

- In-depth content, maps, and advice on a variety of outdoor activities, including hiking, climbing, biking, scenic driving, and wildlife viewing.

- A free monthly E-newsletter that delivers the latest news right to your inbox.

- Our popular games section where you can win prizes just by playing.

- An exciting and educational kids' section featuring online quizzes, coloring pages, and other activities.

- Outdoor forums where you can exchange ideas and tips with other outdoor enthusiasts.

- Also Falcon screensavers, online classified ads, and panoramic photos of spectacular destinations.

And much more!

Point your browser to www.FalconOutdoors.com and get FalconGuided!